DON'T FISH UNDER THE DINGLEBERRY TREE

(And Other Philosophies Of Life)

DON'T FISH UNDER THE DINGLEBERRY TREE

(And Other Philosophies Of Life)

by

Robert Hitt Neill

Mississippi River Publishing Company
P.O. Box 391
Leland, Mississippi 38756

Library of Congress
Cataloging-in-Publication Data pending

Produced and Designed by Betsy Harper
Jacket Design by Cliff Ruminer
Illustrated by Cliff Ruminer
Technical Assistance provided by
Leland Printing Co., Charles and Debra Reeves, Owners

Published by Mississippi River Publishing Co.
P.O.Box 391
Leland, Mississippi 38756

Printed in the United States of America

10 9 8 7 6 5 4 3 2 1

ISBN 0-9617591-9-4

Other Books By Robert Hitt Neill:

THE FLAMING TURKEY

GOING HOME

THE JAKES!

THE VOICE OF JUPITER PLUVIUS

HOW TO LOSE YOUR FARM IN TEN EASY LESSONS
AND COPE WITH IT

This book is dedicated to Beau Neill, and to Dude McElwee, and

Gary Dye

S.P. Crockett

Ronny James

Gene Drake

Semmes Ross

Eustice Raines

In appreciation for thirty years of outdoor and indoor fun

Since those times when our Rebels were Number One!

CONTENTS

ARRANGING AFFAIRS

DEAR DANNY,

I ENJOYED YOUR RECENT LETTER INFORMING ME OF your successes in the field this past season. It is always good to hear from the younger generation, in affairs of the hunt as well as the heart, and I hope you get the latter back to normal also, now that turkey season is over.

I must assume that the only reason you would have to mention your fiancee's remark that "she considered dating other boys during turkey season and she didn't think I would even have taken notice," and then include her lovely picture, is that you wish me to render advice concerning the situation. I am truly honored and humbled, and pledge to apply all my accumulated wisdom to the matter. It is far too seldom nowadays that a young man will turn to his elders for counsel.

Moreover, it is quite commendable of you to foresee this potential problem in an otherwise happy engagement, and to go to great lengths to forestall it. Obviously, you must make the proper arrangements to keep your bride-to-be content, well in advance of next spring's season. My hat is off to you, sir.

It is readily apparent that you must find a substitute to accompany your lady to dances and other events during turkey season. Since you intend to marry this girl, obviously the stand-in should be someone trustworthy who also is a sportsman and will show her a good time. Yet there is always a danger that she might become attracted to the stand-in during a season of almost two months, including scouting trips. This must be a careful choice. Should she fall for the substitute, I assume you'd all remain friends, and that you would wish the happy couple well, as well as visiting often.

Alternatively, you may be tempted to consider having her squired around next spring by someone large and ugly, but I don't advise this, for two reasons. In the first place, you love the lass and want her to have a good time, therefore you cannot place her with a dullard. She'd blame you, not him. In the second place, if you obtained a large ugly person with a sterling personality, and the two of them had a wonderful time together for two months, you might be injured severely in attempting to retrieve your fiancee. Remember, *never* fix up your girl with a man who is bigger, uglier, and meaner than yourself!

So, what are your choices for a sporting substitute?

Though you have a beautiful young lady, it should nonetheless be obvious that no turkey hunter worth his salt will be willing to provide temporary stand-in services during the spring. The only possibility might be one of those guys who shoots turkeys from the road with a rifle, and both of us know what a poor influence that sort would be on her younger brothers. I'd almost as soon have a golfer pick up your date. No, I think we must look elsewhere for this candidate.

Yet we must be careful about whom we consider for the duty; I hate to admit it, but certain types of hunters cannot be trusted in this situation. For instance, all big game hunters tend to regard life as a series of challenges to be conquered. This is acceptable as far as mountain goats and grizzly bears are concerned, but certainly not with your fiancee! Besides, big game hunters usually have more money than they know what to do with, and you might return from the turkeys to find a future mate who has become accustomed to a Cadillac life style, while yours will continue to be a Chevy for years to come. Trust me on this one: no big game hunters.

We probably should also stay away from those sporting types who make a habit of groping around in the dark, like coon hunters and frog giggers. Groping is fine in its place, but that place is not in a dark car with the woman you plan to marry!

Now, I know a few duck hunters who are fine fellows; and duck hunters have a remarkable amount of free time these recent years. However, I have heard it on good authority that true-blue duck hunters are not the warmest of companions for young ladies. Something to do with all those years standing waist-deep in ice water, I understand. We must think ahead here, and cover all possibilities, with her welfare in mind as well as yours. Suppose she fell for the duck hunter, married him (with your blessings), and later wanted children? For her sake, let's examine other fields of endeavor.

Quail hunting is a gentlemanly sport, and that season ends in time for a bird hunter to conveniently arrange such an affair as you suggest. But bear in mind that bird hunters are not used to doing much for themselves; it's the image of their sport. They have people to saddle the mules, train the dogs, pull their tall leather boots off at day's end, clean the birds, cook supper, and mix the drinks. I have to raise the question: would such a person (gentlemen all!) have a tendency to sub-let this responsibility, too? Suppose that, unbeknownst to you, your quail hunting friend hired a large ugly person to escort your girl?

I also have noticed of late that quail hunters, at least those of my generation, are wont to sit around in the evenings sipping very good whiskey or cognac and spend infinite hours talking about "how it used to be." As I understand it, that's precisely the problem you need to correct now: "But Danny, we used to have fun together until turkey season started." Let's keep looking.

Dove hunters, alas, have gone the way of the mule and hand-picked cotton: there ain't no more, except a few fair-weather first-weekenders. In the old days, a dove hunter might have been your best choice, though. They're pleasant, accommodating types, and throw bodacious parties! However, the younger generation doesn't seem to have the per-sistence necessary for long-term relationships, either with doves or girls. Sadly, many dove hunters have been seduced by the party life, and have become golfers. They're into doves solely for the Opening Weekend, and are back on the course by the following Wednesday afternoon. Remember, you're after a stand-in for nearly two months!

Do you get the feeling that we're close to the bottom of the barrel? Stay with me here; faint heart never won fair lady!

Now, I have the same objection to inveterate deer hunters that I have to squirrel hunters: they all seem to chew tobacco, or worse, dip snuff. Haven't you ever wondered what happens to the cud when (or if!) a deer hunter kisses a girl? Don't forget, we're only talking about a two-month substitute here. Would you want to return after turkey season to find a date now addicted to snuff? I thought not.

To their credit, deer hunters will stick with a cause; if you did have to resort to one, I could almost guarantee that he would be on time for every event your lady wanted to attend during the whole of turkey season. As long as she didn't mind the cud in his mouth. Maybe you could ask him not to kiss her good night?

Another thing: deer hunters usually drink beer or cheap whiskey, and yell a lot. A quail hunter might bore the light of your life talking all night, but at least he has quality tastes and courtly manners.

Have you considered a fisherman? Not a bass fisherman, of course, that would roar in one side of the dance and out the other at 75 mph, like those guys do. Ladies like a little time and tenderness, for goodness sakes. Now, if you should happen upon a bass fisherman who knows what a sculling paddle is, he might be worthy of an interview. Don't misunderstand me here; I'm not suggesting that he use the paddle on her! It's just that maybe some of the old-style, take-your-time-and-enjoy-life bass fishermen might still survive in isolated pockets of the universe. If so, check to see if he's already engaged.

I could not, in good conscience at least, recommend a trout fisherman. I've never been real sure about men who walk uphill to go fishing, know what I mean? However, they can be very mannerly, and are generally clean and neat. Yet I'd still be quite uncomfortable with one loose in the neighborhood. Also, he might be afflicted just like the duck hunters from standing around in all that ice water for an even longer season.

I happen to know a real nice white perch fisherman, though, who usually has time on his hands during April while the river is too high to fish. This is a jig fisherman, not a minnow man. Quiet, patient, sensitive touch with the hand—you know the kind; he might be just the ticket. I consider him a good younger friend, and will be glad to speak to him on your behalf.

Of course, you could always teach your girl to turkey hunt and take her with you, couldn't you?

No, I take that back. The first season that she bagged three gobblers with ten-inch beards and all you killed was a scrawny, eleven-pound jake she'd never let you forget it, and a beautiful marriage would end in either divorce, or murder.

Better go with the white perch fisherman. I'll let you know what he says next week.

> Sincerely,
> Uncle Bob

HEY, I WAS NERVOUS
THE FIRST TIME, TOO!

BETSY AND I WERE IN THE WOODS ALONE FOR THE first time in over two years, slipping along from tree to tree. We were mainly enjoying being outside, though I had my 30.06 along. Our marriage was a year and a half old, we had a brand new daughter, and I was home on leave after sixteen months gone where the United States Navy, in its infinite wisdom, wanted me to go.

When a small buck stepped out of a paw paw thicket about seventy-five yards away, I wasn't particularly excited; any deer I took a shot at today was going to be a nice one. We froze next to a big pecan and watched as the deer strolled across the December woods, staying in the shadows. Since my rifle had a two-and-a-half power scope, I offered it to my bride. "Here, Bets, you want to look at him through the scope?"

Well, of course she did, so she shouldered the gun, but it was stocked for my longer arms. "I can't see a thing," she whispered, moving her head back and forth. "Nothing but black," she complained.

Suddenly the buck stepped out into a sunny clearing, and I realized I had underestimated the dark antlers in the shadows. This was a nice buck!

I counted eight or nine points. The deer was only forty yards away, quartering across in front of us.

"Hey, that's a good buck! Gimme the gun," I exclaimed.

"No, I want to shoot him," Betsy whispered enthusiastically.

The buck must have been deaf, for he never paid us the slightest attention. "Go ahead, then," I ordered impatiently.

"I can't see him!" she ground out, still moving her head up and down the stock. The object of our conversation was still moving steadily away.

"Shoot or gimme the gun," I urged.

"Still can't see him," was the anguished reply.

The buck was now ninety yards away, and finally seemed to sense our presence. In the last clearing we were going to get, he stopped and looked back, still unalarmed. "Gimme the damn rifle!" I exclaimed, reaching for the 30.06.

Suddenly, "I see him!" "Boom!" said my wife and my gun.

I saw the deer squinch up momentarily, then take off like a bat out of hell. "You hit him! Shoot 'im again, baby! Shoot 'im again!" I cheered.

"I can't! I've got my eyes closed!" was the reply.

To give her credit, she had never fired a high-powered rifle before. The deer was out of sight before I could either get her eyes open or get the gun away from her.

It was lucky we found him. Betsy had made a great shot—right though the heart—but he ran 150 yards without dropping a drop of blood. He had gone in a straight line, and I walked right to him. Sure enough, he had a pretty nine-point rack.

Out came the camera, and we took pictures until the film ran out. Betsy was as proud a hunter as I've ever seen, until the moment of truth came.

All the mirating was over, and I pulled out my scabbard knife. I flipped it, caught it by the blade, and offered it to her with a smile.

"What's that for?" she asked suspiciously.

"That's to gut him with. If you don't field-dress him, the meat will spoil."

"Well, you do that," she replied.

"Can't. The rule is, everybody has to dress out their own deer, especially the first one. Bad luck not to."

"I don't know how," she pointed out.

"I'll instruct you. It's easy. See that right there? You start by cutting around that, then you pull out...."

"That's bloody and messy and I don't want to do it!" She sounded pretty firm about this departure from The Sporting Rule Book. Matter of fact, damn firm.

I have made some good deals in my life. I once sold a soybean crop for $9.80 a bushel, and got 85 cents a pound for my cotton one year. I bought a Ruger .22 Magnum pistol gunbelt with a real quick-draw holster for forty bucks when the owner was moving to a city that forbid pistols. I was a charter member of the Dude McElwee Crankbait of the Month Club. But this deal today was to be the deal of a lifetime!

Remember that we had a brand-new daughter at home. I had been exposed to dirty diapers for maybe three weeks. Enough.

"Okay," I conceded, still holding out the knife. "I'll make you a deal. I'll clean all your game from now until forever—if you clean all my babies."

She agreed immediately.

In all, I've changed perhaps a dozen dirty diapers on our three, which are at this writing college age or older. Best deal I ever made. You might say life-changing.

(Editor's Note: Babies are usually in diapers for about two years, so the three have totalled six years of changing diapers. As of this writing, the Neills' marriage has lasted twenty-seven years. That weights the trade pretty much in favor of the wife. Since that time, the wife in question has killed several deer—all with one shot each—and numerous doves, squirrels, and other game. And will probably continue to do so!

Betsy Neill, Editor)

Ironically, my own first buck had been killed less than a half-mile from where Betsy got hers. Big Robert and I were coming in for lunch, meeting Big John at the road, when we heard the dogs coming toward us in a real hot race. Daddy handed me his 30.06 (I had a shotgun) with the instructions, "Run head 'em off. Holler if you get anything."

I topped the second ridge to see a herd of deer topping the third ridge, headed my way. The herd buck was a big eight-point, and I snap-shot him just like a dove. He reared up, then fell in his tracks, heart-shot. I raced to his side, and got the shakes. He was beautiful! I opened my mouth to yell, as instructed.

No sound came out.

I tried again. Nothing. I heard Big Robert yell, then Big John's "Reckon he shot himself?" when I couldn't reply. Then the sound of grown men in hunting boots running toward me. Big Robert burst into sight, huffing and puffing. Before he even inspected the buck, he roared at me, "Dammit, boy! Why didn't you yell?"

"Daddy, I couldn't," I squeaked out. Big John exploded into laughter, dipped his hand in the blood, and smeared my face.

"Hell, Robert, don't you remember your first?" he chuckled.

There was another Robert, two generations later, who had just the opposite problem. This was a kid that my daughter Christie (the infant in the first episode) brought home from Tulane. He took to hunting with the rest of the Jakes like a duck to water, and it was just natural for Adam to put him in a deer stand when he showed up for Christmas holidays. Dude even loaned him his 30.06, and I instructed him on how to hit a running deer. Adam and I made the drive that morning, and heard Robert shoot. He was on Adam's side of the swamp, so I'll have to let him tell the story.

"I knew it was Robert when I heard the shot, so I hurried, in case he had crippled one and needed help. As I got closer, I could hear a voice, obviously carrying on a conversation. 'Reckon he's shot somebody else, and is talking to them,' I wondered?"

(We later realized it was a real commentary on the kid's inexperience that nobody ever considered that the other person might have shot Robert!)

"Whoever he was talking to, it was non-stop, so I started running. Sure enough, when I broke out of that cottonwood thicket, I could see Robert standing over there by the big honeysuckle patch, just holding forth. I yelled, and ran to help with whatever first aid was needed. But there was a seven-point buck in the vines, dead as a hammer! Not seeing another soul, I asked him who he was talking to.

"'Why, the deer,' he said, as if it was the most natural thing in the world to hold a loud conversation with a dead deer in the woods.

"Actually, it was a blessing, I soon realized. Because then he switched from the deer to me! The whole time I was gutting the deer, bloodying his face, and dragging the buck to the edge of the woods, he was talking non-stop. It's now my theory that he never hit the deer atall with the

gun; he just talked the poor thing to death! What a way to go!

"The only time he shut up was when he finally asked me to light his cigarette for him; he was shaking so bad he couldn't even strike a match. I lit the thing, and Robert's inhalation was so powerful that I literally saw the cigarette turn to ashes in one draw. Shhhhhoooopppp! And it was down to the filter!"

Robert undoubtedly deserved a prize for first-kill pride. Whereas most hunters wash the blood from their face as soon as they get to soap and water, this kid wore it for three days. We had to make him wash his face!

Bloodying a rookie hunter's face is an old and honored tradition, but sometimes there's a variation on that theme. And sometimes it's richly deserved.

Jerry Center came to the island as my guest after Thanksgiving one year. While he had been a fraternity brother of mine years before, he had returned to Ole Miss for law school, so was a classmate of Beau's, too. He and Beau came into camp after classes let out, so they were a couple of days behind the rest of us. It didn't take them long to catch up.

They weren't even halfway to camp when a nice eight-point ran across the road in front of them. Beau slammed on the brakes (which, wonder of wonders, worked!) and hissed at Jerry to take the shot. Neither of them had even uncased their guns.

This was Jerry's first deer hunt, and he had bought a brand-new Winchester 30.30 for the occasion. The buck stood and watched from twenty-five yards while Beau sweated and Jerry fumbled for his rifle, then for shells, then to figure out how to load the gun, then to cock and aim it. Finally, the rookie hunter had a bead on the buck's heart as the deer stood still at twenty-five yards, and pulled the trigger.

The bullet hit the buck's hindquarter.

After much yelling and chasing and five more shots, the excited hunter had his first buck. Beau helped field-dress it, mopped a handful of blood across Jerry's surprised face, loaded up in the Ghost, and drove to camp. It was a really good buck, and the celebration that night was quite enthusiastic, by all hands. Even to the point of several toasts. More than several, by some.

Especially the Great White Hunter. By the time supper was over, Jerry was telling anyone who'd stand still how he had downed the deer with one shot through the heart as it ran through the canebrake like a striped ape. When he posed with his new gun by blowing imaginary smoke from the barrel, like an old west gunslinger, one of his elders had had enough.

"Huh. Anybody who'd shoot a deer in the butt ought to have his own butt bloodied!" Uncle Sam declared in a meaningful voice, looking directly at me and S.P.

The two of us took the hint and slipped unnoticed out of the cabin. All the deer were in the cooler, an old refrigerated truck body that we had converted to a gasoline motor. We picked up one of those big milkshake cups as we left the porch, and opened the cooler. S.P.'s big ten-point had been in there for two days, and the blood partially congealed inside the open body cavity was nearly ice-cold. We dipped out a gracious

22

cupful; it runnethed over, matter of fact, Biblically speaking.

When we re-approached the cabin, Jerry was on the porch, bending over helping Clyde Abercrombie skin a squirrel. Center's small, and S.P. is bigger than I am; Crockett simply swung one leg over Jerry's back and straddled the bent form, facing rearward. He wrapped his arms around the smaller waist, and popped the little butt up in the air. I grabbed the presented waistband and jerked jeans and skivvies down to the knees.

Then, as Uncle Sam and the rest of our bored-to-tears mates cheered, I poured that ice-cold blood sloooowwwlllyyy down the exposed cleavage.

"Oooohhh! OOOOhhh! OOOOHHHH!!" the rookie screamed. "That's *cold*!!"

There was no mercy in anyone's heart tonight. The bragging had gone on too long. Uncle Sam reached over and pulled Jerry's jeans back up, and gave him a good-natured pat on the rear. "Congratulations! You're now a real deer hunter!" he grinned.

Oh, yes, we did take pictures of all the trophies, as usual. And the last time I was in Jerry Center's den, there was his eight-point mounted over the gun rack holding that Winchester lever-action. And in a golden frame right beneath the rack, hung the trophy picture from that night: grinning from ear-to-ear, Jerry was posing under that same rifle in the cabin rack—proudly holding up a pair of bloody skivvies!

THE INSIDIOUS MOVE
TO BAN FISHING

IT IS NO SECRET THAT I BEGAN WRITING AT THE encouragement of my wife ("Find something else to do with your hands and leave me alone!") and two friends, Mac and Virginia Gordon. Mac was editor and publisher of what we fondly called "The Weekly Wiper" back then, and they rented the house next to us for a year, becoming true Brownspurians...Brownspurious...country folks.

Virginia was down at our house one post-Thanksgiving evening having a toddy with Betsy, while I was away at deer camp. (It is in the Bible that all Southern Christian men *must* deer hunt between Thanksgiving and New Years. We don't necessarily enjoy it, but duty is duty.) The Assistant Editor, Business Manager, Advertising Executive, and Lay-Out Editor of *The Progress* made the innocent remark, "I wish we had something outdoorsy for the paper." At that time (1985) I was a closet writer, pure and simple, and had been for twenty years. Betsy was the only one who knew I wrote as a hobby.

So Betsy reached over in the desk drawer, pulled out a few legal pads with my penciled chicken scratching on them, and said, "Here. See if you like this stuff."

And Virginia did. Therefore, Mac started running my stories. Therefore, a whole new life got started for the Neills, for better or for worse. It's better than farming.

So, I am deeply indebted to the Gordons; all the more so because Mac doesn't even hunt. He is a...golfer!

Previously, I had been convinced that golfing was one of the first visible symptoms of AIDS. Now, however, I was beholden to one. Surely, I thought, there must be some redeeming features to the game that I have overlooked in my ignorance.

But there weren't.

Mac and I have, all in fun of course, crossed editorial swords at the drop of a ball since that time. The article that followed one such exchange even won a national first place award. The letter below was generated by Mac's caustic aside to me (and thereby all other hunters and fishermen) in his column touting the economic benefits of a (shudder) local golf tournament.

Dear Editor,

Last week you saw fit to throw the gauntlet at the feet of our area's sportsmen, claiming that golf is more beneficial economically than hunting and fishing. I respond to your slurs, in hopes that you will share your editorial page—matter of fact, since you oft times complain of having to fill your weekly space, perhaps this could even run under your byline?

I reply in cold, hard facts, not passion, and all figures are approximately accurate, rounded off to the nearest million or so, give or take a couple. This should prove that the hunting and fishing industry is what really keeps our community alive, and that golfers contribute little or nothing to the local economy, other than their usual constant carping and agitation.

For example, town sporting outlets sold $14.6 million worth of shotgun shells, rifle cartridges, fishing lines, baits, rods, paddles, life jackets, boots, and all the other myriad accoutrements of sporting life over the past few years. During that same time period, they sold sixteen golf balls. You ever see a worn-out golf ball? Or club? And nobody even *sells* golf clubs locally, though it's been rumored that Ralph Jennings would part with his for little or nothing on some days. But could that possibly benefit the whole community?

In any store that handles clothing items, you can find camouflage, but where in town can one purchase, or even steal, those loud, fancy britches that golfers wear? Is there a black market operation over in Scratch Ankle?

Our community drug stores sell vast quantities of insect repellant to sportsmen, especially during turkey season, but a mosquito is a discriminating insect that has never been known to bite a golfer, though there have been instances of them biting AIDS victims. In addition, pharmacists sold $6.2 million worth of Band-Aids, Ace bandages, Ben-Gay, aspirin, antiseptic, sinus remedies, antibiotics, and related medical items to sportsmen during the same period that they sold $81.27 in sunburn lotion and $2.9 million worth of Alka-Seltzer to golfers. Again, the hunters and fishermen are tops.

When local men leave for hunting camps or fishing trips, they go to our grocery stores and spend $9 million yearly on sardines, rat-trap cheese, crackers, R-O-C's, Vienna Sausages, an occasional steak, and maybe even a beer or so. Golfers spend $6,723.95 yearly on pretzels locally. Along that line, the principle claim to golfing fame seems to be in the amount of beer soda guzzled on the 19th hole. Yet I will wager that more of that grocery item is consumed at the East Side Country Club by hunters and fishermen on a rainy afternoon, than by golfers at the West Side Country Club on any two sunny days. Also, I have it on good authority that beer soda is delivered to the West Side Club by tanker truck directly from the Beer Soda Brewery—at no value whatsoever to the local economy.

Hunters, by contrast, use petroleum products by the tanker truckload, but bought piecemeal and locally: in their trucks, jeeps, outboards, ATVs, etc.—even on their guns! Golfers use electric carts. Again, no benefit to our community.

Sportsmen even keep our town's professionals in business: look at the number of broken teeth this first year of having to use steel shot for ducks, for instance.

And our doctors state that they use thousands of stitches a year sewing up cuts, bullet wounds, or fishhook accidents; they use the equivalent of two concrete trucks as plaster for casts on fishermen who slip and fall in their boats; and they treat an average of 583 cases of pneumonia just during the duck season. Thirty-year records at the old Witte Memorial Hospital show only one golf-related accident; an infected hangnail from opening too many beer cans.

Attorneys also benefit: the number of divorces during turkey season triples each year. Also, many wives of hunters have been known to shoot their husbands (again, especially during turkey season!), whereas my legal research reveals that no golfer has ever been similarly dispensed with. Which must lead one to the obvious conclusion that they "ain't worth killin!"

Bankers thrive on hunters and fishermen, financing jeeps, bass boats, lakeside cabins, hunting lease purchases, and the like, while gleefully foreclosing on homes and farms during turkey season. Never in recorded history has a man lost his farm by playing too much golf. Never.

After discussing these cold, hard facts with our city fathers, they have decided to outlaw golfing, and at next Tuesday's meeting will vote to either lease the golf course to Perrin Grissom, Jr. for a cotton farm, or sell it to Alton McIntire for a housing development.

(Good Lord, Mac! You don't think anyone except you will take this seriously, do you?)

For Better Journalism,
Bob

The good-natured comments following mine and Mac's exchange led to the idea for the national award-winning article that followed:

FISHING OFTEN FATAL; SPORT TO BE BANNED

In a recent press conference, heads of several government agencies announced a move to ban fishing, according to a Reliable Source (except for a continuing doubt as to whether he really caught that nine-pound bass from Morgan's Pond on rod and reel!)

"Statistics show that fishing is evil, nasty, hazardous to one's health, and often fatal," declared Reed D. Fineprint, head of the Occupations for the Safe and Healthy Associations (OSHA).

"The fish many times suffer permanent lip damage, and are otherwise adversely affected, if not mortally injured."

Supporting his statement was Ms. U. Betta Eachaprunes, of the Food, Drug, and Alcohol bureau (FDA), who said, "Research reveals that exposure to sunshine causes cancer, and fishermen usually sit in the sun. Our agency recommended years ago that canopies be installed on boats, yet these people consistently refuse to protect themselves. Fishermen have also been known to consume vast quantities of alcoholic beverages, developing cirrhosis of the liver in many of the specimens we have examined.

"In addition, the fish are often fried in oil, which raises cholesterol levels, resulting in heart attacks and strokes for those who eat fish," she enumerated. "Too, studies have shown that many fishermen, while on trips, grill steaks for supper, and charcoal-broiled steaks are known to induce cancer in rats. Sex is also known to cause cancer, and surveys seem to indicate that fishermen engage in that activity, at least enough for the procreation of the species."

"OSHA regulations expressly forbid sex for anglers in canoes," Reed D. Fineprint interjected sternly.

"Many fishermen chew tobacco and spit in the lake," pointed out Ms. Ree Sonably Pure, from the Environmental Protection Association (EPA). "In our tests, laboratory mice bathed six times a day in tobacco juice developed wrinkled skin, turned brown, and died within five years. Obviously, this pollution must be brought under control."

"Crime statistics are clear, in that more fishermen are killed by their wives for coming home late than any other group except turkey hunters," commented Ray I. McCool, head of the Federal Bureau of Instigation (FBI). "Our problem is that many states, especially in the South, do not consider husband shooting a criminal offense. Since we cannot solve the shootings under the legal system, we support this move toward preventive action."

McCool continued, "Limit and license violations are also common among these so-called sportsmen, and we'll solve that problem by simply outlawing the sport itself. In addition, fishermen often have outboard motors stolen, creating criminals. We feel that banning fishing will reduce crime significantly."

Moe Fineprint, brother of Reed and administrator of the Infernal Revenue Service, stated his agency's position: "By their very names, we feel these people are evading taxes. Anglers are obviously looking for angles to avoid payment. Many of them also hunt, making them guilty of Hunting For Angles, a clear tax violation. This step is long overdue, in our opinion."

"We will be eliminating untold suffering throughout the nation," declared Ms. Pure. "Just think of all those poor roaches, crickets, minnows, and worms; they will no longer have to face impalement on a hook!"

"And those hooks are dangerous, sharp instruments," pointed out Reed D. Fineprint. "Countless fishermen and innocent bystanders have been injured by them."

"Yes, and the resulting infection from those gooshy worms and roaches has proven fatal to a significant portion of our population," said Betta Eachaprunes. "As a matter of fact, all our studies, taken together, clearly reveal that the mortality rate is one hundred percent for the sport of fishing: fish, bait, and fisherman—they all die sooner or later. We must act to counter this alarming trend!"

One of the interested public attending the meeting, later identified as the proprietor of Charlie Pignatelli's Pizzeria and Bait Shoppe, pointed out that fishing was a form of recreation, and wanted to know what steps the government would take to replace the stress-reducing qualities of fishing.

A Reliable Source (except he never caught no sixty white perch in an hour last Saturday!) reported that at this question, the agency administrators went into closed conference, whispering nervously among themselves.

After some obvious discomfort by panel members, FBI head Ray I. McCool finally fielded the question. "Well, we were not quite ready to announce this, but plans are to eventually ban not only fishing, but other dangerous sports. It goes without saying that hunting is often fatal, too. Hockey, football, basketball, and baseball produce more injuries each year than the Viet Nam Conflict. These sports cause my agency innumerable problems with gun control, drugs, gambling, and illegal immigration. The public has no concept of the amount of bureaucratic paperwork involved in political asylum for a Cuban shortstop who is able to bat .350 and steal one hundred bases a season."

"Both horse and auto racing cause forms of pollution," declared Ms. Ree Sonably Pure of the EPA. "Ping-pong balls and tennis balls are filled with hydrocarbons, which when released make holes in the ozone layer. We must put an end to this threat to human life on the planet."

"Pool balls have been known to cause intestinal blockage when swallowed by alligators," observed FDA chief Ms. U. Betta Eachaprunes, "and these reptiles are an endangered species."

"It is therefore our intention to outlaw all sports except golf," finished Reed D. Fineprint of OSHA. "Golf is healthy; the participants ride around in pollution-free electric cars, stand in the shade, except for brief moments on the greens, and drink healthful quantities of cholesterol-reducing Lite Beer."

"Never in legal history has a golfer been killed by his wife, as so often happens to fishermen," Ray I. McCool pointed out. "In fact, there is ample testimony in divorce proceedings to the effect that golfers 'ain't worth shooting!' We'll reduce crime by making golf the new National Pasttime."

Moe Fineprint, Reed's brother, was the lone voice of caution among the agencies represented. The IRS chief read a prepared statement urging more study before implementation of the Sports Ban. "We must be able to assess the economic impact on the nation's tax base before moving further on this matter. Most people don't realize that 98% of America's billionaires are playing baseball, basketball, football, or are members of Congress. I have to ask: if we eliminate all these high sports salaries, will we then have to consider taxing Congressmen?"

"Congressmen are taxing enough!" Ms. Ree Sonably Pure retorted heatedly. "As a matter of fact, the EPA is evaluating research that seems to show that the Greenhouse Effect is measurably worse during the months Congress is in session. We are considering making the Administration file an Environmental Impact Statement before another session." After a moment, Ms. Pure regained her self-control and returned to the subject at hand. "We support the Sports Ban at EPA. For one thing, golfers wear those loud yellow britches and bright shirts. We believe that chewing tobacco and snuff will no longer be an environmental problem. Golfers cannot risk staining those yellow pants and white shoes with tobacco juice or dribbling snuff down their shirt fronts like fishermen, bowhunters, and baseball players."

33

"This is a significant move toward a happier, healthier, safer America," declared Betta Eachaprunes. "No more violence; no more getting nasty hands from putting worms on hooks; no more dirty clothes from sliding into second or tackling a running back on a muddy field. No more viennie sausages, like those uncouth hunters and fishermen used to eat! Has anyone *ever* witnessed a golfer eating viennies or sardines?"

Reed D. Fineprint of OSHA stood, indicating that the press conference was at an end. "Ladies and gentlemen, we appreciate your attendance. Any further questions will be taken up at the Nineteenth Hole."

You heard it first right here, folks!

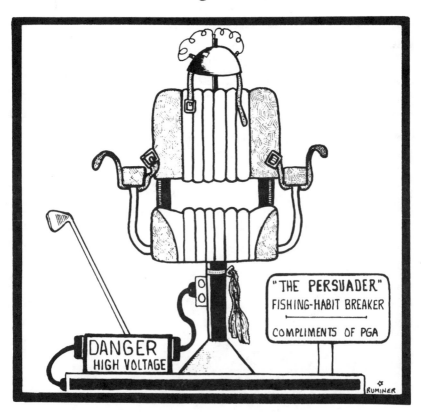

OXBOW BREAM

"DADBLAME THE DADBLAME COTTON PICKIN' luck!!!"

"Bob, I think Dude just lost another leader. How many more flies you got?"

I looked in my little clear plastic box sitting beside me on the bow seat. "I've got two more, and then I'm out. Give him one of yours!"

Fred McDonnell, seated on the middle seat of the twelve-foot aluminium boat, patted his shirt pocket and shook his head. "Not me. I've only got one left."

The subject of this exercise in generosity and agitation glowered at us from the stern. "I don't want anything else from y'all except *quiet!*"

Fred and I grinned at each other as our exasperated partner tied on his last popping bug and little black trailing fly. We three were spending the day on Lake Whittington, an oxbow lake north of Greenville, fly fishing for bream. However, the Mississippi River had crossed us up.

Normally a fly fisherman practices his art (and it *is* an art form!) by sculling slowly along one side of the lake casting toward the bank, with the open lake behind him. There's nothing to interrupt his backcast. It is usually a rather quiet, relaxing, sport: the quick flip of the wrist that brings the line from the water; the hesitation as the rod tip comes straight up and the backcast arcs gracefully out behind; the slow, aiming, deliberate twist of the hand as he shoots the lure toward the next target; the calm, almost whispered, "Nice cast; oughta get one," from his boat partner; the sucking sound of the feisty little bluegill as the popping bug disappears; the grunt of satisfaction as the hook is set and the eight-foot rod bends nearly double. The line cuts almost audibly through the water as the colorful, hand-sized fish makes its bid for freedom. The noisiest time is generally the brief splashing at the side of the boat as the catch is swung aboard, and then the clatter of cold-fish-on-warm-aluminium until the muttered, "Gotcha, you little devil!" right before it is strung. Of course, there's also sometimes an occasional expletive at this point as the catchee fins the catcher in a final stab at freedom.

Today, though, we were being treated to more than an occasional outburst of frustration. We were having to fly fish up in amongst the willow trees that normally line the lakebank. This meant that there was no room for a backcast. Fred and I had adopted a roll-casting technique, which basically involves using less line and maneuvering your rod tip in a circular motion to flip your lure into the desired location. As I have implied, Dude was less than adept at this method today. It didn't help that his partners were missing few opportunities to bring this to his attention.

The Mississippi River was really the culprit for his misfortunes. These "oxbow" lakes are so called because they are one-time bends of the Mighty Muddy that were in years past cut off from the main channel by the ever-changing current; or by the man-made efforts of the Corps of Engineers, attempting to tame the Father of Waters. Nowadays, the government agency keeps the channel stabilized and the oxbows are permanent fixtures, yet they are still connected to the main river at its higher levels, and so are subject to its fluctuations.

The Mississippi was fluctuating now, and the normal shallow water bream fishing areas were inundated by a recent five-foot rise. But summertime usually means that fish are biting *somewhere*, so dedicated anglers stuck to their tasks, and finally the word was spread across the Delta: "They're biting up in the willows!"

Lest the uninitiated jump to the conclusion that oxbow lake bream climb trees, let me hasten to interpret: this meant that the rising waters had flooded some of the many willow "flats" that surround the lakes, and the bluegills were feasting on the insects and grubs that had inhabited the woods. The problem that fishermen now had was to present the bait to the fish, as we were finding out.

Every now and then we would glimpse another boat back up in the shade with us. All these other fishermen were using the age-old bait-fishing technique. With ten- or twelve-foot cane poles rigged with line, cork, sinker, and hook baited with worms or crickets, they were not anywhere near as vocal as our party was. During the day we passed boats containing two or three middle-aged men, older couples, fathers with sons or daughters, and a pair that was obviously grandfather and grandson. Theirs was a laid-back method of angling. It's not often that fishermen get to ply their avocation in the shade, and the folks on Lake Whittington were making the most of it that weekend.

I could not help remembering, as I observed these more tranquilly occupied craft, Robert Ruark's Old Man's axiom to The Boy that fishing solved a lot of problems because "Water cleared the head, fishing calmed the nerves, and you could always eat the fish." Having recalled that, I turned to share this homily with my companions, but then thought better of it. Dude had one foot on the back seat and the other on a tree branch, stretching to retrieve his precious last fly from a willow limb.

Just to test his balance and reflexes, I made two stokes with my paddle, nudging Fred first. It's fortunate that the three of us had been friends a long time, for if we had taken his subsequent remarks to heart, our feelings might have suffered. As it was, the two of us in the boat were able to laugh these utterances off and encourage our companion in the tree to make a suitably humble apology before we would allow him to reboard our craft. Fred had the presence of mind to remove the other paddle from Dude's reach before his descent from the tree. Isn't it wonderful that fishing is the kind of sport where good friends can enjoy each others' company, remember old times, and create new memories to add warmth to the hearths of our fires as we grow older?

We took a needed break and I passed a couple of cold beverages to my companions while Fred opened cans of sardines, viennas, and Polish (pronounced as in "shoe polish") ham. Dude rummaged in one of his tackle boxes and came up with crackers and a ball of gouda cheese. Pocketknives at the ready, we attacked this

"jungle-lunch" with gusto. Surely, when we all get to heaven, St. Peter will give us a respite from the milk and honey routine now and then and break out sardines, crackers, and gouda cheese!

After lunch, we reassessed our little black fly situation, which was at the critical stage. Dude had his last one on, Fred had one extra, and I had two. We'd have to fish carefully if we wanted to make it through the rest of the afternoon.

Of course, we could have re-rigged our fly rods with corks and sinkers and gone back to the bait shop for worms or crickets. But the fish were hitting fine on our popping bug and black fly offerings, and we had assumed that we started out with an adequate supply of flies.

Many bream fly fishermen use only a popping bug, but we have had most of our luck over the years with a small, black sinking fly trailing about a foot behind the floating bug. When the bream are on the beds, sometimes you can use two or three flies behind your bug. I once saw Big Robert, on a bet, tie four flies on and catch five bluegills at once using this tactic.

We always take more than one fly; since oxbows are subject to the Mississippi's fluctuations, they are also subject to the river's debris. After spring high water recedes, there's no telling what is under the surface where that big bream bed was last year. The little black flies snag a lot of bream, but they also seem to snag every stick in the lake.

Dude finally got the hang of roll casting, and the noise of agitation quieted down considerably as the action began to pick up. Several times, all three of us had bream on at once, and Fred, who was officer-in-charge of stringing fish, had to call for a temporary truce to catch up. I broke out some more cold drinks as Dude sliced three more wedges of gouda cheese. "This is more like it!" he grinned, good humor restored.

Fred raised an eyebrow at me. "That ain't what he said an hour ago when he was hanging out of that tree!"

Stringing completed, we finished our drinks and reached again for our fly rods, each down to one fly now. Dude lost his a few minutes later, but not to a tree. A grinnel, or bowfin, that must have weighed six pounds, smashed his popping bug and came slap out of the water when Dude set the hook with his now-famous technique, the McElwee Hoist. We all thought it was a bass at first, so Fred and I reeled in to help our companion. Boating a big fish in heavy cover is tough enough with a bass rod and seventeen-pound test line; with a fly rod and two-pound leader on a bream hook, you need a lot of help—and luck!

Dude skillfully played the big fish down and led it to the boat. We didn't have a net, so Fred reached down as the grinnel broke the surface. He jerked his hand back quickly. "Teeth!" he exclaimed. "Look at those teeth!"

"Dadgum grinnel, Dude," I observed. "Lemme get a pair of pliers." But the fish had played with us long enough. He surged away from the boat, rolled against the leader, and broke free. Dude began to castigate us.

"Biggest fish of the day, I fight him down, bring him right up to the side of the boat, and what do you sissies do? 'Oh, Mama, he's got teeth!' Heck, all fish got teeth. Why didn't you just pull him out?" he addressed us in mock disgust.

Fred shrugged and picked up his fly rod. "I don't like to eat grinnel anyway," he explained.

Dude's knife was on the seat by his hand. As Fred began to shake out line, his leader swung by

Dude's end of the boat. Quick as a flash, the blade shot out and severed the monofilament right behind the popping bug. "What're you doing?" came Fred's dismayed cry as the disattached little black fly sank.

The guy in the back of the boat smirked and chuckled evilly. "Now two of us are outa flies. You wanta explain to Bob that it's time to go clean fish?"

We went to clean fish.

*   *   *   *   *   *   *   *   *   *   *

Fred pushed his chair back and sighed contentedly. "I may can beat the boy fishing every now and then," he observed to me, "but I'll never be able to beat him filleting bream with an electric knife. And nobody in the world can best our Uncle Dude when it comes to frying fish!"

All in all, it had been a good day. Next time I'll just take more little black flies!

Fred

DON'T FISH UNDER THE DINGLEBERRY TREE
(And Other Philosophies Of Life)

IT'S FUNNY HOW SOMETIMES THE BASS WILL BITE during the hot part of the day in August, and sometimes they just flat get the lockjaw. You never know unless you're out on the lake with them. When Christmas Tree Lake used to have all those willows in and around it, we were always able to catch them somewhere, most any time of the day. Dude, S.P., and I even went out at night once; we'd take turns chunking big topwater lures at where we figured the bank was, then be real quiet and listen. If we heard a splash, the next guy would cast; if not, the lure obviously was in a tree and we'd break out a flashlight to look for snakes during plug retrieval.

However, the population explosion amongst the beavers, plus the acid rain, Greenhouse Effect, Lyme Disease, and holes in the ozone layer, not to mention polar icecap warming, killed most of the willows. Now it was a hot little lake, and more often than not the bass were afflicted with the lockjaw. Those of us who fished it regularly had to learn where the holes and dropoffs were, and even had to resort to fishing with those plastic worms now and then.

Cotton-picking season was late one year, due to rain-delayed planting the previous spring, so I got to fish a little later than usual, right on into September. One afternoon an older, wiser companion and I were sculling (well, actually, I was the one doing the sculling) up the campside bank, casting, when I heard a steady "plopping" sound coming from around the bend. "Plop, plop, plop" in the water. I figured it was either a big bream bed, or else the bass were on a feeding frenzy, right around the corner. Speeding up, I saw the water rippling with activity under a familiar bushy tree that hung out over the lake. The short tree was covered with unfamiliar brownish berries; obviously I had not fished late enough in previous summers to notice the fruit.

"Aww Righhhtt!" I exclaimed to my boat partner. "They're tearing it up under that tree. Let's go get 'em!"

My elderly companion was unimpressed, pointing out that the surface activity was being caused by the wholesale dropping of those little brown berries into the still water. "Yeah, but all that ought to be stirring up something that makes the fish bite there," I declared. I cast under the bush and began reeling in.

My comrade sighed and opened a beer. "You ain't gonna catch nothin' there," he prophesied sourly. "Wastin' our time."

"Hide and watch!" I responded cockily. I switched from a yellow Bomber to a chartreuse

Buzz Bait. "I bet they'll take a topwater lure in a Memphis Minute."

"Not hardly," he replied. "Not under that tree."

Well, turned out he was right, but I was determined to prove him wrong. He drank two beers and ate a wedge of gouda cheese while I cast everything in the tacklebox but the needle-nose pliers under that durn tree. Finally I gave up in disgust. "Okay, why don't you try, smarty-pants?" I reached for an R-O-C and the ball of gouda.

He shrugged and handed me a drink, plus the sculling paddle. "Never catch no fish under them trees," he declared.

I sliced a wedge of cheese and picked up the paddle. "What kind of tree is that, anyway?" I asked as we began to move.

"Son, I call that a Dingleberry Tree. Now, you're young, and I'm old, but you can learn something right now that took me most of my life to get ahold of: Never fish under the Dingleberry Trees of life!"

Though I had pretty well gotten over being young at that point in my life, ignorance was still running rampant across certain sections of my gray matter. "What the hell is a Dingleberry Tree?" I asked, still smarting at the rejection of my offerings to the fishes.

"Well, boy, a Dingleberry Tree is obviously a tree from which Dingleberries grow."

"Shoot, I coulda figured that out; but what the hell's a Dingleberry?"

"Son, you've led a sheltered life, whereas I been durn near ever'place I ever wanted to go, and a bunch of places that never had crossed my mind. I have 'heard the owl and seen the elephant.' Lots of times a definition of something depends on where whoever you're asking is from. 'Cornbread' to a European more than likely means bread made with what we call wheat. 'Gay' means one thing in California, and something else entirely in Mississippi. Or at least it used to," he remarked glumly.

"I came over here one time fishing with a fella, but it started raining before we ever got to the lake," I recalled. "I mean cats and dogs! We decided if it ever let up during the night, we'd get up and try 'em for a while. He was sleeping on the top bunk under that clear fiberglass roofing, and about two he leaned over, said, 'The moon's out, darling,' and went right back to sleep. Boy, you talk about being rudely awakened! He claimed he never said it, but we didn't go night fishing, and I guarantee I never slept another wink. He's straight, but the rest of that night, the California version of 'gay' was on my poor little innocent mind!"

My elder rolled his eyes. "Lordee, what's this world coming to?" He shuddered involuntarily and reached for another beer. "Son, you know I ain't a prejudiced person. Black, white, yellow, red, man, woman, or yankee: they're all the same to me up front. I go by what a fella says and what he does, and I been known to kiss ugly ladies. But there's some places where you got to draw the line. Boy, don't never go fishing with a man whose shoulders don't move when he walks!"

I finished my gouda cheese and picked up my casting rod again. Aiming my red-and-white Shannon Spinner at a stump's base, I chunked and began to reel. "So, back to the original question. What's a Dingleberry?"

Seeing we were nearing a steeper bank, my partner reached for his glasses and tied on a Christmas Tree Water Dog. "Maybe they're deep," he muttered. Chore finished, he closed the tackle-box lid on lures and glasses, adjusted his drag, and rared back to throw. The sparklely bait landed just beyond a log, and he pursed his lips in caution until he had flipped it out of danger. A couple of quick turns to force it deep, and he slowed his retrieve while he spoke.

"Well, down here, most men think of a Dingleberry in terms of being gone to deer or turkey camp for a few days. It's a condition that usually develops from being too long without hot showers and inside plumbing." He grunted as he executed the McElwee Hoist, but it was obviously in response to the Water Dog running over a submerged object. Reeling in quickly, he cast back into the same place. "If in doubt, stick it. If you miss, give it another chance," he quoted the famous outdoorsman.

"Prob'ly a stick," I observed. If it had been a strike, it was the first of the day.

Sure enough, he reeled in empty, and cast again. "Anyhoo, women and children are not equipped for the Dingleberry experience," he declared. "We were speaking a minute ago of males who aren't real men, and I know you've heard the old expression, 'he ain't got a hair on his hienie' which denotes that whoever is being spoken of is somewhat less than macho." He grinned. "It has been my observation that females and chillen don't have the problem. I'd ask your opinion on the subject, but I seriously doubt that you are qualified to comment."

"Aw, I don't know about that," I began.

"I do," he stated firmly. "But you're beginning to get the idea, I hope. After a week on deer camp, most men work up a pretty good collection of Dingleberries. Point is, the condition can be cured with a good cleansing. It ain't terminal."

I did have a strike that time, I thought, as my lure bumped down the side of a log. I cast back toward the base of the downed tree; too hurriedly, for my spinner hung on a root. I muttered a few choice mutters at it as I sculled into the only place we had found a fish in the past hour. "Is there a point to all this?" I hoped as I disentangled the hook from the root.

"I was hoping you'd ask that," he snickered. "Son, you want to learn from this. It ain't no use atall in fishing under the Dingleberry Trees of life. Near 'bout ever'body gets caught under Dingleberry Trees at some time or other. I mean, stuff just 'plop, plop, plop's all over and around you. It might be a bad job, or a mean boss, or a foreclosing banker. It might be a girlfriend or wife that does you dirt and then rubs your nose in it. It might be a bitchy acquaintance or former friend that wants to smear your good name with whatever he or she can find that's stinky and smearable. But whatever the situation, remember: you ain't got to stay under their tree and get plopped on. Get the hell out of Dodge, as the old saying goes."

"You will recall that I am presently in farming, which is about as much directly under a Dingleberry Tree as one can get, for a lot of us in these days and times," I pointed out. "Once you're in, there usually ain't no way to get out, even if you want out. And that occupation is fast getting over being fun."

"Exactly!" he crowed. "Now you're beginning to catch on. If you get caught under those Dingleberry Trees, and just stay there, it can change your whole outlook on life. Lookee here; how many folks can you name that been caught in just the farm crisis, and they flat ain't no fun to be around no more?"

"I ain't got that many fingers," I sighed. "But I understand what you're saying. I've had good friends that got wedged into bad business situations, or legal problems, or poor marriages, and became completely different people."

He nodded. "They fished too long under their Dingleberry Tree, right? I think you can see what I mean. Son, you got a good sense of humor, you're fun to be around, you scull pretty well, you're big enough to tote what somebody my age don't want to tote, you ain't bad to drink atall, and you will clean the fish as long as I agree to fry them. Helldamn, you're even going to wash dishes tonight and bring me coffee in bed in the morning!"

"Don't push it too far," I warned, grinning.

"See there? You gotta admit I got a better deal fishing with you than old Freddie Fodrod. But if your situation in life begins to get you down, that grin won't be there any more. Folks who stay under the Dingleberry Trees get whiney and bitchy and grumpy and..."

"And Dopey and Happy and Sneezey and Doc," I interrupted. "Hey, but sho'nuff, I see your point. I just don't see how you can get away from it sometimes. You can't just throw up your hands and quit every time life gets tough and starts pitching curveballs on the outside corner. Or, in the present vernacular, every time you pass under a Dingleberry Tree."

"I never said that. There's ups and downs in ever'body's life, far as I know. But when those times come, you keep your sense of humor, and you damn well do what you can to change things for the better. Fish a different bank, or cast out in the middle of the lake. Crank the motor, or pick up the paddle. You may not get immediate relief, but make up your mind not to fish under that Dingleberry Tree any longer than you have to, and if finally the only way out is to get out of the damn boat, then hold your nose and jump. But come up smiling, glad to be out from under! Don't let it ruin your outlook on life."

Any further conversation was cut short when my partner's rod suddenly bent double. He set the hook with a grunt, and hossed the bass from between two stumps. As long as he had him coming, he kept the pressure on, while I grabbed for the net. Wouldn't you know that his beer and the gouda cheese were sitting atop the net, which was lying on the middle seat. I tried to catch the cheese, as the beer spilled through the weave, and therefore missed my initial stab as the too-green six-pounder went under the boat. My comrade desperately stuck the rod-tip under water, but it was too late, and the line parted with an audible twang.

"Damnation, boy! You done spilt my beer, dropped the cheese, and let the biggest fish I've had on in a month get away! What the hell..."

"Whiney, bitchy, grumpy...I see what you mean," I said with a nod. "You want to go back to camp, keep on up this bank, or go on fishing under your own little Dingleberry Tree?"

He took a deep breath, exhaled slowly, and opened his beer-splattered tackle box to look for another Christmas Tree Water Dog. After a minute or two, he shook his head and muttered, "Plop, plop, plop...."

I grinned and picked up the paddle.

*   *   *   *   *   *   *   *   *   *   *

This conversation comes to mind now and then, but never as clearly as the weekend after my third book came out. I was feeling good, I mean. *The Flaming Turkey*, my first effort, was already in reprint in less than a year and had been named Runner-up for Best Outdoor Book of 1987; the farm book, my second one, was selling well five months into the marketplace; I had just achieved national distribution; *Going Home* had been delivered and

51

looked great; and the light at the end of the tunnel no longer appeared to be a speeding train.

That weekend was also the opening of deer season, and Betsy took matters into her own hands, as she does so often, thank the Lord. "One more day isn't going to make a bit of difference as far as shipping all these orders out," she declared, "and you really need to take a break and go to the woods. Just bring home some venison."

"But, hon..." I half-heartedly began to protest.

"No buts!" she said firmly. "The kids and I will take care of packing and addressing orders tomorrow, both UPS and the Post Office will be closed Sunday, and we can have everything shipped out by Monday evening anyway. I've got your duffel bag packed. Grab your 30.06 and we'll see you Sunday night. Good luck!" She kissed me and shoved me toward the gun cabinet.

Was this Heaven, or what?! Man, I was flying high!

I was getting into the truck when she stuck her head out the door. "Honey, before you leave, could you check the john in B.C.'s bathroom right quick? It seems to be kinda sluggish."

At seven-thirty that evening, I was digging up the septic tank to try to get the durn line unstopped. Around nine-thirty, I ended up sticking a fire hose down the sewer line clean-out in exasperation, turned that sucker on full blast, and then tried unsuccessfully to dodge quickly enough. Eventually the hose did the trick, but not before a goodly amount of the mess had "plop, plop, plopped" all over me. I remembered that lecture in the boat years before as I stripped down to my skivvies, clamped the lid back on the septic tank, resolved to shovel the dirt back over it Monday, and went to shower. I arrived at the cabin sometime after midnight, my previous high mood all shot to hell. I did not kill a deer; seems everything shied away from my stand for the whole weekend, despite my shower.

No, I didn't stay under that Dingleberry Tree; I fished on down the bank and found another good sunny spot to cast in. But I did uncover another perspective.

You ain't really a hot-shot until you can hire someone else to clean out your sewer line after dark on the night before deer season opens. Until then, you've still got something else to work toward.

And hopefully, one day you can laugh about the times when life stunk!

Uncle Sam

Beau

Bob

CLEANLINESS IS NEXT TO WHAT?!!!!

THE GREAT OUTDOORS IS NOT A PARTICULARLY clean place, as most of us who venture outside know. There's sand, weeds, dirt that turns to mud or dust with the whims of the weather, bugs, spiders and their webs, and other impediments to Clean Living to be encountered just on a short hike into the woods. On camping expeditions, or even a simple church outing for the evening, the campfire smoke always stings one's eyes and pungently scents hair, clothes, and equipment. Ashes on a hot dog, sand on the marshmallows, and bugs in the stew are Outdoor Givens. A fishing trip of only a couple of hours requires that one's hands become tainted with the intimate inside juices of worms, crickets, roaches, and even the fish themselves. Cleaning game after a successful hunt involves both sweat and blood.

As the saying goes, "It's a dirty job, but someone's got to do it!"

Hunters, fishermen, campers, hikers, and canoers often will leave civilization and force themselves to endure these conditions for days, or even weeks, at a time. Now, while there are some camps which are Cadillacs, so to speak, many

55

others are just Edsels and Studebakers, where conditions are relatively primitive. There ain't no room service, much less inside plumbing.

These conditions are understood and accepted by most outdoorsmen; indeed, sometimes they are unnecessarily harkened back to. For instance, I was never allowed to forget the time we first installed running water and a hot water heater in our rustic cabin. After five days of deer hunting, I showered, shaved, and splashed on smellgood before we broke camp and headed for home. Took three months to allay her suspicions, and I've never shaved on camp again!

This type of misunderstanding is a wonderful justification for including the ladies in the outdoor activities, if possible. If your wife will accompany you on hunting trips and suchlike, I encourage you to make arrangements for her participation. However, I must warn those husbands who enjoy the comfort of a cabin out in the boondocks: wives view such fine accommodations with their own precious feminine viewpoints, bless their hearts.

A lady will enter a comfortable cabin that may have just been cleaned, and judged as such, by every male occupant present, and declare: "Good Lord! How can you live in all this filth!" There's no sense in getting upset about it, guys; she really does mean well. Women are just different from men, and praise the Lord for it!

My suggestion in these cases is to plan on arriving at camp by at least the middle of the afternoon before Opening Day, endure her expected outburst with a suitably guilty expression, but explain that you must depart for the woods to scout the hunting area before nightfall. She will be perfectly content in your absence, scrubbing and dusting things that you scrubbed and dusted yourself last turkey season. Just remember to be very complimentary about the spotless cabin upon your return.

Scrubbing your own body is an activity that really is called for at times during camping trips. For instance, a fellow gets up in the cold dawn, dons long johns, insulateds, flannels, woolens, and other clothes designed to keep him from freezing, and heads for the woods. By noon, a warm front has come through, the temperature is up to sixty, and our hero has a 150-pound ten-point buck to drag out to the road.

We're talking major sweat here; and for an extended period of time. Then the buck must be loaded into the jeep and, since the weather has turned warm, must be skinned out back at camp, quartered, and the meat packed into ice chests for preservation. By this time, the afternoon hunt is nearly over, and someone has to catch up the hounds, feed the horses, cut some firewood, and start supper. After three days of this type activity, you could swear that a family of skunks has set up housekeeping in the bottom end of your sleeping bag.

But the sleeping bag itself is not the problem; it is merely a symptom. Bedding can be aired during the day and made tolerable. It is crawling into that bag with yourself that becomes intolerable.

Beau and I reached that point one November on deer camp and vowed that we were going to bathe in the Mississippi River, in spite of the fact that the water temperature was a chilly fifty degrees. Armed with soap, towels, and clean clothes, we cranked the jeep and headed for the riverbank sandbar. Bear in mind that this was miles from any coeducational civilization. Just a couple of us boys around, and an occasional tow-boat in the river channel, which was maybe 250 yards away. At that distance, no one could even determine gender, much less detail.

We shed our clothes and long johns at the jeep and, with soap and towels, walked to the river's edge. The plan was to lather up good in the ankle-deep water by the sandbar, then run out to greater depth, submerge, rinse, and run back to our towels, thus minimizing exposure to the cold river water. As we began working up a lather, a towboat rounded the bend upstream, unnoticed by us, though it made no difference to The Plan because of its distance. Finally, sudsy from head to toe, we pitched our soap toward the jeep and turned to the water. "Last one in is a rotten egg!" I bellowed. We charged into the river, anticipating the cold but cleansing shock.

And kept charging. Unbeknownst to us, the dog-gone sandbar was only ankle-deep for nearly 200 yards.

"Yeeeeeee-haaaaaaa!!" Our Rebel Yells attracted the attention of the towboat crew as we sprinted through the shallows, suds flying. The forward lookout waved toward the bridge, pointing.

"Yeeeeee-haaaaaa!" we yelled, knowing the next step would surely be deeper. The Captain moved to the starboard wing and raised his binoculars.

"Yeeeee-haaaaa!" still ankle-deep, we charged. The deck crew lined the starboard rail as the towboat's whistle blew a salute.

"Yeeee-haaaa!" I could feel the suds drying as we raced onward. The ship's cook stepped from the galley, wiping her hands on her apron.

"Yeee-haaa!" was sounding hoarse and forced as we ran. The Captain's wife joined him on the wing of the bridge and reached for the binoculars.

"Yee-haa!" was becoming a scream of desperation as goose bumps pushed soapsuds from our bodies, while what seemed to be the soprano section of the Mormon Tabernacle Choir began emerging from the crew's quarters.

"Ye-ha!" What next?

Mercifully, less than fifty yards from the tow-boat, our feet finally hit deeper water as the crowds cheered. We raised our heads from rinsing just in time to hear the first mate bellow, "Whatever it was, it ain't chasin' you no more!"

We sprinted back. Cleansed.

Yet, once the hunters' bodies are fully cleansed from the rigors of the trip, there remains a job that usually falls to the lady of the house. It is not really fair that all those filthy garments must be rendered acceptable for polite society again by one who does not regularly enjoy the trips, but sometimes a wife and mother learns the hard way not to trust her menfolks with complicated household appliances.

It was actually a rather natural thing to do, I tried to explain to calm down her down. Matter of fact, most teenage boys would have been had up for being helpful beyond the call of duty, I pointed out. Surely she appreciated the situation wherein a couple of dove hunters who had been caught in the rain thought better than to just leave their sopping hunting shirts in the middle of the floor? How many youngsters would be considerate enough to stick the wet camo shirts in the dryer, saving their mamas all that time and trouble?

To be honest, it had not been the boy who had done the deed. However, I learned a long time ago that when the lady of the house reaches a certain degree of temper, it is usually best to blame things on someone who is out of reach. In the present case, Adam was now over a hundred miles away at college. Discretion is sometimes the better part of valor, and I could always 'fess up after she cooled down.

Doves are different from most game birds in that they are about two hundred percent feathers. These feathers are just barely attached to the bird's body—a hunter can literally blow on his limit of doves to pick them, except for wing and tail feathers. Many retrievers only work on doves under protest, for the feathers come off in the dog's mouth so easily. Yank used to deliver my doves reproachfully, afterwards spitting out wads of distasteful gray fluff. The fact that this loose attachment is really an advantage in dove cleaning was completely lost on my big golden Labrador.

It was also lost on Betsy when she opened the dryer. One dove had been overlooked in one pocket of one shirt by one hunter.

This dove was now completely picked, ready for easy cleaning and cooking. However, my instincts told me that it would probably not be to my best interests to point this out to my wife, at least not right now. Yet it has since occurred to me that there may well be a new commercial application here. I mean after all, what else does that Maytag repairman have to do?

If one does not hunt doves (or is not married to a dove hunter), one could not imagine the amount of feathers in that dryer. They burst out when the door was opened; they permeated (and penetrated!) all of the clothes; they stuck out from all those little holes in the dryer where I guess the hot air comes in; they packed the filter in layers. I was later to learn that skivvy shorts washed with dove feathers cause embarrassing itches in places that cannot be scratched in dignified company.

Since quality outdoor books usually include some tips on game cookery for their readers, perhaps I could offer the Neill Family Recipe for Dried Dove:

One (1) Dove; uncleaned, but freshly deceased

One (1) electric clothes dryer

One (1) small load of men's underwear (freshly cleaned)

Note: Women's underwear might work just as well as far as the dove is concerned, but I suspect would greatly multiply the number and coverage of embarrassing itches, perhaps leading to the liberation and burning of these garments.

CAUTION: Do not use long johns!!

Directions: Place dove and underwear in dryer under low heat for one (1) hour or until the filter stops up. Remove dove, dress (not in underwear), and roast on grill for twenty (20) minutes wrapped in a strip of bacon.

Donate underwear to Salvation Army (notify your accountant for proper tax deductions).

Clean filter.

By the way, this recipe also makes for an interesting side dish: Steamed Wife!!

WOODS VEHICLES

WE WENT OVER TO THE ISLAND FOR THE
afternoon not long ago, and I was once more
reminded that one of the main reasons men go to
the boondocks is not to hunt and fish, but to have
an out-of-the-way place to work on our woods
vehicles. There would be no fun atall in trying to
fix a recalcitrant four-wheel-drive when women
and children are present. Or preachers.

Big Robert never felt that he had been hunting
if he had not bloodied his knuckles working on the
Ghost or the Green Scout. He'd crawl up under
the vehicle with an adjustable wrench (also called
a knucklebuster) and a hammer (a hatchet would
do in a pinch) and proceed to bang merrily away
on the thingamajig or the whatchamacallit. Then
he'd talk to it for a while, until finally the machine
would begin working again. Uncle Sam, however,
always seemed to get nearly as good results by
simply talking to it, and never bloodied his hands.

With woods vehicles, brute force is often pre-
ferred over skill and knowledge, at least to start
with. For instance, Dude and I once proved that
one can indeed change the flat on a Scout by
removing left-handed lugs right-handed. I will
admit to a subsequent problem in trying to keep

the fresh wheel on, but it just goes to show that there is very little a couple of good strong men can't do if they really set their minds to it.

Caution should be used in some cases, however. Big Robert once aimed an aggravated blow with a ball-peen hammer at a rusted-on wheel rim, but he got the rubber tire instead and the rebounding peen hit him squarely in the forehead, knocking him cold. And I have observed several broken toes, fingers, and hands from the unwise application of brute force.

Sometimes the brute force doesn't even apply, however. There's a perfectly good index finger somewhere on Montgomery Island that became separated from its former owner by simply checking to see whether the fan belt on a jeep was tight enough. After the flow of blood was staunched (yes, the belt was plenty tight), the man commented rather dejectedly, "I knew better than to check it while it was running." He had worked on farm machinery for forty years, so he sure did know better.

It's not always mechanical problems that beset woods vehicles. I have observed four-wheel-drives so stuck that it took three days to get them out. I cannot count on both hands the number of times I have gone hunting or fishing, only to spend the better part of the day trying to get a jeep out of the mud or sand. Again, this is part of the fun of being in the outdoors, and woe is the hunter who cannot get decently stuck even once on a weekend hunt. That's a sign of a closet golfer.

Our womenfolk are usually not as understanding about these situations, though. Nothing throws a wet blanket on a stuck outing party like a young lady who sits sphinx-like in the front seat and wants to know every five minutes, "Are we having fun yet?"

As much as we talk about, and talk to, our woods vehicles, though, when it comes down to the lick-log, every hunter will generally champion his own with the phrase, "Best vehicle on the island!" You can get in trouble making fun of another hunter's woods vehicle. I can well remember the time when Beau and I were headed across the river while our cousin James was having one more with a couple of other hunters on the levee.

"Y'all go ahead. I'll be right on behind you. I know that old Ghost of y'all's won't crank, so I'll be there in a few minutes to push you off with my jeep. Y'all ought to shove that old Ghost in the river!" he agitated.

Beau and I just looked at each other and cranked the outboard. We motored across and put our gear and guns in the Ghost, which cranked on the first try. We then made a quick, unobserved stop by our cousin's jeep before heading on to camp three miles away.

A couple of hours later, we heard a disturbance coming down the road that warned us to temporarily vacate the premises. Moments later, James came wheeling precariously into camp, steering with a pair of vice-grip pliers. Red-faced, he hailed Big Robert, who was innocently sweeping off the porch.

"Where the @*#*!! are them two boys of yours?! They done stole the damned steerin' wheel off my jeep!"

We stayed out of sight until he cooled down, then gave him back his old steering wheel, with appropriate remarks. But he never dared to publicly taunt the Ghost again.

Undoubtedly, the words that get most jeep drivers in trouble are the words, "Aw, heck! We can get through that spot a'flootin' and a'flyin'!" I first heard them from Jim Pat when we were following Jim Brown and Clyde Gault headed for an all-day rabbit hunt. Well, Pat didn't say just exactly that, but it was more or less the same thing: "Aw, heck! They made it okay, didn't they?"

We never turned the beagles loose. Got stuck at seven in the morning, and got out at five in the evening.

Ronny James and Mom Raines stuck the Ghost in much the same way coming off of Woodstock one afternoon. They were so late that Big Robert had passed the mad stage, and was seriously worried. Since making that observation, I used the same tactic myself in later years, having learned that when temper turns to anxiety, the stuckee in question usually skates by without lasting damage, physically or vocally. And having just written that, I think I understand that my kids have used it on me.

Keeping a woods vehicle in the boonies sometimes makes for unexpected surprises. I was once the first member to arrive at the riverbank vehicle park on the island for spring turkey season. It was unusually warm, and when I flung the tarp off the Green Scout I was prepared as always for wasps; therefore I didn't panic at the five-foot snake coiled around both ends of the dashboard gun rack. "Chicken snake," I muttered, grabbing him by the tail and slinging him into the road. Immediately, inspiration struck!

Fred Bordelon had been loading his boat when I left the levee landing, so I knew he'd be next behind me; and his jeep was right across the road. I quickly re-caught the snake before he could get out of the road, and approached Fred's jeep. Sure enough, it was unlocked (his had doors and a top). I opened the door and introduced the ungrateful snake to his new abode, which didn't seem to suit him at all. Before we parted company, he managed to bite me on the little finger, and then squirmed out of sight under the driver's seat. I shut the door and turned away, grinning. This was gonna be fun to watch!

Until I looked at my finger. Blood oozed redly from two holes across the middle knuckle.

I've been snakebit by a cottonmouth, a copperhead, and countless garter, king, chicken, and rat snakes, not to mention puff adders and farming. I knew that poisonous snakes left two holes, and non-poisonous snakes left a horseshoe-shaped mark that rarely drew blood.

And I knew damn well that the snake in Fred's jeep was a chicken snake.

And chicken snakes make horseshoe-shaped bites.

And my bite was bleeding from two places, about a half-inch apart.

But chicken snakes *do not* have fangs.

Moccasins, rattlesnakes, and copperheads have fangs, though.

Yet I *knew* that snake was a chicken snake.

Yet I knew chicken snakes make horseshoe-shaped bites.

Luckily, Fred stopped to chat with some other hunters on the levee side, because it took me over a half-hour to get that damn snake back out of his jeep for certain identification. I mean, I looked in his mouth and down his throat!

Yes, it was a chicken snake.

This may be the only information of lasting value in this book, so I want you to pay attention here: LARGE chicken snakes can bite completely across one's little finger, so that the bony jaw cuts on each side of the knuckle, while the front teeth, so to speak, never touch your skin.

I hope Fred reads this book, otherwise he'll never know how close he came to getting a real scare that day!

Everyone knows that while I have had my moments with snakes, those are calm, well-considered scares, not panics. Everyone also knows that what really panics me in a vehicle (or anywhere else, for that matter) are wasps—in close proximity, of course. That's why I prefer open-air woods vehicles, so that one of us can make a quick exit. And I ain't really particular as to which one of us.

Sammy Shaifer used to keep a dark green jeep station wagon on the island, and it stayed in really good shape until the time I'm thinking about. He and I went over for deer camp one fall, and nobody had been in his jeep since before ginning season. It cranked right up, and we were maybe halfway to camp when the heater finally got to warming things up good.

Including at least a jillion red wasps which had built nests in the heater vents.

Suddenly there were clouds, swarms even, of big ole mean nasty red wasps pouring out of the vents. I was lucky Sammy wasn't driving too fast, but that would have made no difference in my decision to bail out. Fast.

In all my days, I don't believe I've ever seen so many wasps in one place at one time, except once. And while not in the boonies, that incident also involved a woods vehicle. Plus an unwanted growth of yucca bushes, up at the schoolhouse.

The durn things are also known as Spanish Daggers, which should tell you something about their personality if you don't have any in your yard. In this case, the schoolmarm was afraid some kid would get an eye put out or something, so she asked for my help in removing them during the summer.

Winches on jeeps are wonderful pieces of machinery. You can not only pull out of a mud-hole when the vehicle is stuck, but you can pull bushes out of the ground. No problem, I assured Susan; I'd just run into town with the jeep and jerk those thorny suckers out of her way by myownself.

So I caught a slack couple of hours one day that week, jumped in the jeep, and tooled into town for a quick yucca-jerk. No one was around the school when I wheeled into the parking lot, pulled up to the edge of the curb, left the jeep idling, threw the winch into neutral, and got out to pull about fifty feet of cable off the reel. No sense in rutting up the schoolyard by driving on the grass. I flipped a loop around the bush, careful not to get jabbed myself, and slipped the end hook around the cable. The loop would tighten around the base of the yucca when I reeled the winch up.

Humming a little winchy tune, I got back into the jeep and hit the winch switch. Sure enough, it worked just like I said it would. The cable tight-ened, the yucca shook and leaned over, and the root ball pulled slap out of the ground and began to drag toward me across the schoolyard. Fifty feet, forty feet, thirty feet—and then I noticed a dark cloud above the bush. At twenty feet, I could hear a buzzing sound, so I switched off the winch.

Wasps!!! The dadblamed yucca was apparently chock-full of wasp nests! Now there were ten zillion wasps swarming above the uprooted bush! I slammed the jeep into reverse and scratched off backwards. The whole town knows how I feel about wasps.

As I backed up in my panic, I suddenly realized that all those wasp nests were still attached, as it were, to my (topless) jeep! At twenty feet, all the wasps were still following their nests around the parking lot, extremely ticked off about being uprooted. I couldn't go forward without winding

up the winch cable, which was definitely not the thing to do right now! Nor could I unhook the cable from the yucca without getting very intimately involved with more wasps than I had ever seen in one place in my life. And after the second circle of the parking lot dragging the yucca, I discovered that the cloud of wasps was getting strung out; I was catching up to the rear of the swarm. There was only one option left: into the street we raced in reverse, still dragging the yucca at a distance of twenty feet!

Followed by a large swarm of angry wasps!

So if you were one of the folks in town that day who observed a backward-speeding jeep dragging a yucca bush around and around the streets while making its way to a certain schoolmarm's house—where, having temporarily outdistanced an angry swarm of wasps, the driver hurriedly unhooked the winch cable from the yucca, reeled it in, and sped away frontwards—well, now you know.

THE SAGA OF
THE SULTAN OF COW BONES
MOUNTAIN

IT ALL STARTED OUT INNOCENTLY ENOUGH, WITH A letter:

Bob:
I see you are going to be teachin' at some fancy writin' conference in Oak Ridge in April. I think we oughta attempt defeatherin' a turk. With two writers on the sneak, I'm sure we can cause one to die...laughing!

Yourn,
Sam

Little did we know that before the Saga of The Sultan of Cow Bones Mountain was over, one of us writers *would* nearly die—but far from laughing!

I had accepted an invitation to hold seminars at the Tennessee Mountain Writers Conference, only twenty minutes or so from the stronghold of Sam Venable, veteran outdoors writer and feature columnist for the Knoxville *News Sentinel*. Venob and I both had beautiful wives and daughters, were admirers of each others' books, and had the same bent toward a humor/nostalgia style. If nothing else, the hunt promised a fun time. I made the call to accept, and my host arranged for a Virginia license.

Being in the eastern corner of Tennessee, Venob was only an hour's drive from hunting in Virginia, North Carolina, and Kentucky, as well as his native Tennessee. For our hunt, we would cross into Virginia to hunt with a mutual friend, Sam Mars III, on private land. This was to be my first turkey hunting experience away from my Mississippi River bottomland swamp country, where levees hold the Mighty Muddy captive during the spring turkey season annual high water. My only reservation about trying a mountain hunt was a reconstructed knee—as so many old college athletes seem to be plagued with.

My usual jinx almost held true. I had already hit the hay the night before the hunt, when a knock sounded in the hotel room. "Your van is sitting on a flat," I was informed by Durrell Hutson, one of the TMWC planners. "It's too late to find a gas station open to fix it, so just take my van to meet Sam in the morning. Maybe I'll bring you luck." She handed me her keys.

So at 3:30 a.m. I was on the way to Venob's house in a strange van, borrowed from a young lady who barely knew me. Did these folks have a handle on Southern Hospitality, or what?! Sam was ready, accompanied by his pretty blonde teenage daughter, Megan, dressed in camouflage. Sam's wife, M.A. (Mary Ann), had made us coffee and returned to bed. We hit the road in Venob's truck for the drive to the Mars place, Megan dozing between us.

The Mars place was durn near straight up!

"Not to worry, old son," Venob puffed as we made our way up the steep logging road in the darkness that fateful morning. "Climbing up a mountain is tough on lungs, not knees." My low-lander's bellows were certainly getting a workout, and I was grateful when Sam stopped partway up for a breather. "I (puff, puff) heard you (puff, puff) pantin' (puff, puff) back there," he wheezed. "I guess (puff, puff) we've got time (puff, puff) to let you (puff, puff) catch your breath." The man was all heart!

"Dad-blame, Sam!" I complained after I could breathe normally once more, "I didn't know folks actually had to *work* to go turkey huntin'. In my part of the country it's mostly fun."

Well, different, anyway. On the River islands, where I had grown up hunting, we usually have to ferry all our supplies in by boat, and get up early enough to take either a boat ride in the darkness, or an obstacle-course-muddy jeep ride for several miles from our cabin to our hunting area. There's maybe only a six-foot difference between a draw and a ridge in the swamps, and I had never even seen a rock while hunting! In the Mississippi Delta, if you find a rock it means somebody brought it with them, and then left it there when they went home. Now, Sam and I had been climb-ing up this one rock he called "Cow Bones Mountain" for nearly half an hour!

"Well (puff, puff), at least it hasn't (puff, puff) hurt my knee," I commented as we stopped at a level bench for our third breather. "How much farther?"

"Oh, it doesn't ever hurt your knees climbing *up*," my guide replied, "it gets them going *down*! 'Lungs up, knees down' we always say." A little diabolical chuckle sounded in the pre-dawn darkness as he said, "And we're fixin' to get to the steep part!"

It is a wise man who knows his limitations. As I looked almost straight up at the next section of trail, I decided that the territory I was presently standing on looked exactly like prime turkey hunting habitat. "I'm gonna hoot from here!" I declared. And proceeded to do so.

Eight gobblers answered! I dropped to the ground and began to crawl toward cover as Venob watched with a puzzled expression. "What the heck are you doin'?" he demanded.

Most of my hunting partners know I'm partially deaf; too much gunfire and a ruptured eardrum. In the swamps, when I can hear a gobble, I know I'm too close. My rule has always been that if I hear a gobble before I hear wingbeats, I blind in right there! The advice I usually followed came from a couple of older hunting companions of my youth, the Brown Max and Mr. Jimmy Rogers: "Find a place that looks like a turkey will walk close to, get hid and be still like if the turkey saw you first he'd shoot you, and call once in a while." Hearing eight gobblers sounding off now put me scrambling for concealment.

Venob regarded me with amusement. "Old son, there ain't a one of them gobblers closer'n a half-mile. Which one you want to go to?"

We split up, me still marveling at being able to hear turkeys gobbling without having to worry about scaring them off. Must be the thin mountain air, I figured. Because for all our work climbing that Cow Bones Mountain in the dark, several of the roosting toms were *below* us! I picked a close one, whispered "Good Luck," to Venob, and headed downhill. I could tell right away that Sam had been correct in his assessment of the effects of down-mountain walking on a bad knee.

Still unable to gauge distance in this unfamiliar environment, I flushed a hen before I realized I was getting close to my chosen bird, which sounded like a real boss gobbler, maybe even that one the two Sams had called "The Sultan." When the hen flew, I plopped down immediately, and crawled to the closest big tree. With dawn approaching, I pulled on my face net, settled old SouthPow at my left hand, and tried in vain to silence my pounding heartbeat. Up the slope, the tom double gobbled on the roost, apparently undisturbed.

Twenty minutes later, I gave a couple of clucks, and got an immediate response. I waited ten more before trying a series of soft yelps. He double gobbled. Now it was light enough to see, and I glanced to my right to pick shooting lanes.

"Holy Cow!" I almost exclaimed out loud. It was nearly straight down! I resisted an urge to use my belt to tie myself to the tree, but did begin to consider how far I'd slide if and when the turkey came up and I shot. Surely the recoil would shove me off the side of the narrow ridge I had sat down on in the darkness. I could just visualize the headlines: "Veteran Outdoorsman Dies In Fall Off Mountain After Bagging Boss Gobbler." Could I move to a safer perch?

The tom gobbled again, ending any speculation about moving, for he was obviously on the ground now, though still uphill. I braced as much as possible with my good leg, took a firm grip on my gun, and yelped a response. Another double gobble.

And it went like that for two more hours. The turkey moved very little, it sounded like, but refused to come closer. A couple of hens went by about forty yards below me, which made me wonder: suppose The Sultan does catch a hen in this terrain? How in the heck was he going to perform without breaking his cotton-pickin' neck?

Suddenly, I had the answer—apparently in a tree. For as I cut my eyes back uphill, a huge, silent, black form sailed down the slope and lit in a tree only thirty yards away. At first I assumed it was a buzzard or large crow (both unusual in the Mississippi Delta), so I was caught with my gun down, so to speak. The bird leaned over to regard me with a piercing eye, and I caught a glimpse of a long, thick, rope-like beard. The doggone gobbler I was working had flown in on me!

And I was more or less flatfooted, my gun on the ground at my side. There was no way I could move with him looking right down my throat. I pretended to be moss on the side of that tree.

The situation stayed that way for probably ten minutes, though it seemed several hours to me. This was the first time a turkey had ever flown in to my call, not to mention lighting in a tree close by. In the Delta, self-respecting gobblers don't do such things. The thought even crossed my mind that perhaps there was an ethical problem here: in Mississippi, we frown on roost-shooting; but this gobbler had been on the ground for two hours, and was now back in a tree at 8:30 in the morning. Surely this couldn't be classified as roosting? Not when he had obviously come to my call and had the supposed hen pinpointed!

Suddenly, the tom double gobbled again, and then—to my total amazement—strutted and pirouetted on the limb!

Ethical problems be durned, I decided. If he did that again, I could get my gun up when he turned his back to me. If Virginia turkeys re-roosted at 8:30, Venob could just tell me about it later.

Sure enough, he repeated his act, and I eased SouthPow halfway up. He regarded me suspiciously, but his ardor won out, and he gobbled and pivoted again. Once more, and my gun was to my shoulder. The next time he stretched his neck to look, I pulled the trigger and grabbed my tree!

Down crashed the huge gobbler, one of the few one-shot kills I have ever made. I dragged myself back up to the ridge and sat on him while he flopped, my heart pounding in rhythm. Now that I had him down, this was a *big* turkey—maybe even The Sultan! My Rebel Yell echoed down the mountainside, informing Venob that his guest had scored.

However tough I had thought walking downhill with a reconstructed knee was before, it was T-U-Double-Uff now, with a gobbler across my shoulder that was rapidly approaching fifty pounds! I was limping badly when I reached the road, but my reception from the two Sams and Megan made it worthwhile.

"That's got to be the big turkey that's outsmarted us so many times," Sam III graciously declared, admiring the over-ten-inch beard. Venob hefted the bird (which weighed twenty-two pounds at the official checking station) and agreed. I couldn't help but remember a paraphrase from Robert Ruark's *Old Man and the Boy*: something about a true friend being the one who helps you brag on your trophy. These friends were working overtime on that job, as they mirated over The Sultan of Cow Bones Mountain.

Those of us who love the outdoors know that the best part of any hunt is the afterglow—the warm memories that remain for decades, and are even passed down to new generations. I had a feeling that this Virginia hunt with the two Sams would prove to be one of those from which legends are born. How right I was!

I had downed The Sultan on Saturday morning, the Writers Conference ended that night, and Betsy and I had driven home Sunday. Much of the conversation on that ten-hour trip had to do with The Sultan (in my ice chest, picked), the two Sams, and my first mountain hunting experience. It made for a short drive.

Wednesday night, the phone rang, and luckily it was me who answered, for the caller didn't even pause to identify himself. "AAWWW-HAAAWWW!" trumpeted the voice, loud enough for Betsy to hear all the way across the room, "You didn't kill The Sultan! I got him today! He was twice as big as that li'l ole turkey you killed! He had a foot-long beard, six-inch spurs, and weighed nigh onto forty pounds! Yours was just a li'l ole jake, compared to mine! I killed The Sultan of Cow Bones Mount!"

"That you, Venob?" I queried. "You been drinkin'? I got The Sultan in my freezer, right now. You musta been in a barnyard today. Look and see if your turkey has a label on its breast saying Butterball."

Seems my partner had gone to the same area of Cow Bones Mountain and called up another big gobbler. "I blasted him right by the tree you were sittin' under, and he went floppin' down the slope, and I jumped on him in true Neill fashion, and me and him fought hand-to-hand for awhile, and I killed The *real* Sultan!" Venob exclaimed long-distance. Was there any need in me asking who was going to be featured in the Knoxville papers that week as the Greatest Turkey Hunter Of All?

As a writer, I sometimes find myself moved to poetry, and here was inspiration to verse, if ever I saw it. The following day, I sent a poem to Venob. It went like this:

THE SULTAN OF COW BONES MOUNTAIN

There lived an old gobbler up on Cow Bones
    Mount,
Had fooled Mars and Venob for times with-
    out count.
Then venerable Venob came up with a plan:
"To capture The Sultan, I'll call in my man!"

"When Neill yelps aloud in that Mis'sippi
    drawl,
The Sultan can never resist that sweet call.
He'll fly down the mountain, and strut on a
    limb;
And if Neill's alert, he'll sure clobber him!"

Oh, hunters from five states did marvel that
    day,
When Neill climbed that mountain, The
    Sultan to slay.
They fought and they bled, and went down
    for the count;
And so died The Sultan of old Cow Bones
    Mount!

The legends of that day soon started to
   spread;
New gobblers moved in where The Sultan
   had tread.
But venerable Venob himself was tough stuff,
And thought that Neill's fame had spread far
   enough.

The gobbler who'd moved to The Sultan's
   abode,
Was tame, and not suited for most hunters'
   code;
But Venob had downed him, and cried, "I,
   not Neill,
Have captured The Sultan of old Cow Bones
   Hill!"

So, fables and legends from which verse is
   made,
Are often determined by scribes, who are paid
To honor the Home Team, and not even
   count—
Neill, slaying The Sultan of old Cow Bones
   Mount!

This poem left Brownspur headed for Knoxville
on Friday morning. A week went by, with no word
from Venob. Then another. When the third week
with no reaction began to drag by, I worried,
"Maybe I didn't know this guy as well as I thought
I did. Maybe that poem made him mad. Maybe..."
But then the mail came, with a letter postmarked
Knoxville. I ripped it open.

Brother Bob:
   Guess where I spent the better part of last
week: in UT Hospital! In Isolation. I came down
with some mysterious bacterial infection, caus-

ing Doc Ferguson to scream, 'Aaarrrgghh! Get your tail to the hospital, pronto! And touch no one enroute!' or words to that effect.

Old son, we both know the meaning of diarrhea and dysentery, but you ain't *never* had nothin' like this! Everything passed, if I might be so bold as to use the term, before me: my life, the final tally of the New York Stock Exchange, the Manhattan Yellow Pages, minutes of the DAR meeting, *everything!*

The lab people finally ID'd it—I am not making this up—as some sort of canine bacterium. A doggone dog germ! (And if that don't crank your poetic mind into high gear, there ain't a turk in the South.) They poured the antibiotics to me and...ta-dah!...I be cured.

Soon as I learned it came from dogs and found out the incubation period, I figured out the source. A week earlier, Megan and I went frog-gigging. One pond was thirty feet downhill from a coon dog lot which, judging by the smell, hadn't been cleaned out in at least two months. Given the powers of rainwater and gravity, you can pretty much figure out where the stuff was running. And given the fact that we were slopping around in the pond—and I was chain-chewing toothpicks, as is my habit—it don't take a PhD to figure out how the cooties got transferred from water to guts.

By the way, how 'bout printing out another copy of your 'Sultan of Cow Bones Mountain' pome and signing it for the Virginia turkey hunters. I want to frame it and hang it in the cabin. It's a masterpiece, even if it is riddled with lies, half-truths, falsehoods, and other gems of outdoor writing!

You're Another One,
Venob

P.S.—I have included the pix so you will know what the Cow Bones Sultan *really* looked like. I call your attention to the following facts:

A) Massive, shin-ripping, man-killing, inch-and-a-quarter spurs;

B) Shave-brush-quality, eleven-inch beard;

C) Wing tips worn to pointy nubs from frequent strutting;

D) General, all-over haggard look brought on by 1) two months of non-stop love making; 2) two ounces of fives to the head and neck; 3) two hundred pounds of Venob performing his patented 'Flying Zambeezi' on a forty-five-degree slope.

Venob

Sam was right: my poetic mind went into high gear. As requested, I printed out another copy of my earlier poem, and sent it to the Virginia hunters, with two copies of its obvious sequel:

THE SULTAN'S REVENGE

The Sultan of Cow Bones Mountain had
    finally met his match;
They'd brought in a pro from Mississippi who
    managed to make the catch.
The Sultan died like a monarch should, his
    lustful cry in his throat.
He died with his spurs on, trying to breed
    just one more litter of poults.

The mountains shook when The Sultan fell,
    from Virginia to Tennessee.
Folks whispered in awe of a man named
    Neill, a great white hunter was he.
But when the mighty have fallen, and
    conquerors have gone home,

Usurpers invade the harem, pretenders make
    moves on the throne.

A lesser tom drummed for The Sultan's hens,
    but quickly was spurned in disgust;
Lovesick, he answered to Venob's call, and
    got number fives in his butt.
The bragging began, and the story was told,
    that this gobbler had been the best;
But the Ghost of The Sultan heard those lies,
    and roused from his peaceful rest.

The Ghost of The Sultan, who ruled Heaven's
    Roost, looked down from the Golden Way,
And spying the scribe who had started those
    lies, declared, "There'll be Hell to pay!"
He went to St. Luke with this horrible tale,
    who said, "Put his guts on a binge.
I've got just the jinx: it's dog-doo, and
    stinks; we'll call it The Sultan's Revenge!"

The Sultan's Revenge was passed to Venob,
    with the aid of a beautiful blonde;
And a toothpick or two full of dog-doo, on a
    night in a frog-gigging pond.
The Green Apple Quick-Step, The Drizzles,
    The Trots—are terms that make mankind
    cringe;
But even a scribe like Sam Venable, can't
    describe The Sultan's Revenge!

Oh, the Ghost of The Sultan still reigns
    supreme, in the wilds of east Tennessee;
And he curses those scribes who fail to pay
    homage, with terrible dread diseases.
Yes, fishermen lie, and deer hunters fib, and
    dove shooters fudge on their shell count;

But tell Turkey Truths, or risk the Revenge—
of The Sultan of Cow Bones Mount!

Once more, the verses departed from Brown-spur headed for Knoxville, and once more there followed a period of maybe three weeks with no reply. Now I had more than one option to worry about: 1) had I made Venob mad, or 2) considering his recent medical problems, had I actually killed him? I decided to enlist a middleman...er, middle-girl.

My note to Megan was brief, and designed to be easy to reply to. I enclosed a self-addressed, stamped postcard, giving her the option of simply

85

checking the correct boxes and dropping it in the mail. It said:

Dear Megan,

I hate to bother you, but I've had no reply to a missive to your dad last month. Please advise me of the situation by checking the appropriate blank:

1) ____Dad's okay, but mad as hell at you;

2) ____Dad relapsed and passed on after receiving your poem;

3) ____Dad's plotting revenge in a poem of his own, which will be completed in 19___.

Thanks,
Bob

A week later the horrible truth came out, as well as the completely unexpected discovery of a budding blonde poet and humorist! In her own hand, Megan had penned:

Dear Mr. Bob,

I'm sorry this note doth seem so short;
Your name, you see, is but a wart
Upon the thumb of my old Dad
(Needless to say, he is quite mad!).

I tried my best to plead your case,
My only reward: a bright, stinging face;
A knotty head; sore throat and arms;
(And I thought high of my slick charms!).

Forbidden to utter "Bob Hitt Neill,"
I understand how horrid you feel.

I took the sickbed of my newly-healed Dad
(He beat me so hard—it really was sad!).

So here I am, in my dark room,
Between my bed and sheet;
Writing the sad, sad saga
Of our sad defeat.

Forgive my lack of courage;
On me, these sores ain't fittin'.
And once again—forgive me
(I admit I was just kiddin'!).

> Luv,
> Megan Venable

I was nearly overcome with grief at the pain I had inflicted on the child by killing The Sultan Of Cow Bones Mountain. Now, I had to try to make amends, and help alleviate her problem. The final poem in this chapter of The Saga of The Sultan went:

COMFORT FOR THE FAIR DAMSEL IN DISTRESS

Oh Megan Dear, I greatly fear, that I've p.o.ed
your dad.
And if that's true, I promise you, I hate to see
him mad.

Most hunters there, they wouldn't care, if
bested by a turk;
But Venob Sam, he gives a damn—it's just
his little quirk.

Yet he's no call—no, none atall—to take it
out on you!

With belt or fist, no blow he's missed; your
    fair white body's blue.

It's not your 'count, that on the mount the
    Sultan snubbed his call
For it was Neill who made the kill, to start
    this versely brawl.

You tell M.A.—from me, you say—(I guess he
    beats her too)
If y'all could sit in Mississip, we'd see you
    safely through.

The law down here is plainly clear: If man
    beat wife or child,
They'll lay him low, with gun or bow—and
    never go to trial!

But never mind, I think you'll find, with
    Turkey Season spent,
That Venob grin will soon begin—relief is
    Heaven-sent!

So, Megan, now I take this vow: If he asks me
    to visit;
T'would cause you pain should I win again—
    so I'll be sure to miss it!

                Love,
                Bob

My intuition had been correct: the story of
this Virginia turkey *was* the stuff that passes on to
future generations—in song and verse! So, tell the
truth, turkey hunters; The Sultan is watching you!!

MIXED BAG FOR DELTA BOYS

"AH, YOUTH!" I SIGHED AS I WATCHED THE FRIDAY night camp-out crowd back out of the driveway, the jeep loaded down with shotguns, sleeping bags, waders, hipboots, hot dogs, buns, and potato chips. It wasn't a very melancholy sigh, I thought to myself as I made my way back to the warm den, sat in my warm chair next to the warm fire, picked up a warm mug, and saluted my warm wife. Age has its advantages, too.

The temperature outside was around twenty-eight degrees, and a ten-knot north wind made it feel considerably colder. The wind was expected to die before dawn, so Saturday morning would break cold and clear, with a heavy frost in the woods and a thin sheet of ice on still water. The wood ducks would fly early on the sluggish creek through the swamp, and when the sun rose, the squirrels would begin feeding in the oaks, pignuts, pecans, and hackberries.

No sense in letting the boys have all the fun, I decided.

"I'm gonna hit the hay, Betsy," I yawned and stretched. "I think I'll get up early and go to the woods. Just to check on the boys."

She smiled and nodded. I wasn't fooling her.

A mile or so from the house, which is six miles from a small Delta town, lie nearly 600 acres of woods and swamp in the bend of an old creek. We've posted these woods for years in order to build the deer population up to a huntable level. Not only has the deer herd increased dramatically, but we've even seen a few wild turkeys. The swamp provides excellent habitat for wood ducks, and the whole area abounds in small game: squirrels, rabbits, raccoons, and possums. I used to predator call in the edge of the trees for foxes, bobcats, coyotes, and wild dogs until a great horned owl nearly scalped me one night.

As a kid, I had practically lived down there in the woods, and now I was seeing the truth of the old saying: "What goes around comes around." For the past few years, Adam and several of his buddies had spent almost every Friday night from November through January camped beside the same old cypress log where I had slept as a boy.

They'd confiscated an old cotton trailer tarp for a north-west windbreak, stretched between two hackberries. In bad weather, they pitched a couple of tents; on clear nights they rolled their sleeping bags out on an old Marine groundcloth. Supper was usually hot dogs or hamburgers, or occasionally some of the game they bagged. On particularly bad nights, Betsy sent them out a pot of chili or venison stew.

Yes, these are modern kids. I've seen a bumper sticker saying, "Teach your boy to hunt and you won't have to hunt your boy." Now, I don't subscribe to that literally, for Beau and I once spent half a day hunting for a young friend on Woodstock Island. Yet I heartily endorse the sentiment it intends. The way things are today, I'd much rather know that my teenager is camped down by some freezing swamp than riding around a city in a warm car.

That next morning was indeed cold, and I dawdled too long over my third cup of coffee. When I reached the woods, it was already daybreak, and I could hear guns booming down in the swamp. Knowing I was too late to make it to the open pocket where the boys were, I decided to slip along the creek and try to jumpshoot my limit. I wasn't a hundred yards from the truck when there was another flurry of shots from the swamp, and suddenly a flock of a dozen woodies rounded the bend from that direction.

It seemed to me that they could have had the decency to at least flare a little as I emptied French Gun at them.

"Water's probably too deep to pick them up here, anyway," I muttered, reloading.

I continued down the creek, contemplating what the future held for older hunters who lose their shooting eye. A trio of ducks caught me totally unawares when they flushed from the reeds to my right, but reflex took over. The lead drake folded, French Gun's barrel swung by the hen, and the second drake tumbled in a classy double.

"No sense in retiring just yet," I thought smugly, my first three shots forgotten as I picked up my limit of woodies.

I beat the boys to their camp and had just built up the fire when I heard their excited voices echoing through the woods. They hove into view, each one carrying a couple of squealers. Adam also had a mallard drake, and Tommy held up a pair of greenwing teal. Mark wore knee-high rubber boots, but was wet to the waist. The others wore waders or hipboots.

"Daddy, there's a snapping turtle down there under the ice as big as a washtub!" my son blurted out. "You shoulda seen that sucker!"

"Y'all sent Mark out to catch it, huh?" I observed as the wet youth began peeling off layers of clothes.

"No, sir. I was going after a cripple and stepped in a stump hole," the boy said sheepishly.

"I told him to wait and I'd get it," drawled Deadeye. "I had to get it anyway after he fell."

"Uncle Bob, we jumped a great big ten-point coming out!" Tommy exclaimed. "Reckon he'll come back this evening if we went and got our deer rifles?"

"Be worth a try," I observed.

Every one of these kids had been through a hunter safety course that I helped teach. All of them had sighted in their rifles from my back yard, and I felt a lot safer with them than I did in any public hunting area surrounded by adult strangers. And not to brag, but these kids all said "Yes, sir; no, sir; thank you, sir; and please." We read so much today about our youth going to hell in a handbasket, but my experience with kids has generally been the opposite. I watched with approval as Adam and Tommy began to draw the ducks while Deadeye helped Mark find enough dry clothes.

Soon the ducks were gutted and hanging in a tree, and the five of us walked out of camp in different directions. The sun was peeping through the forest now, and bushytails were on the move. I eased south a couple hundred yards to a big sweetgum den tree I knew about. It was in the middle of a grove of oaks, most of which bore those big overcup acorns. As I slipped toward the den tree, a black squirrel moved on a lower limb, and the shot was a cinch. I leaned against the sweetgum for an hour and killed three more red squirrels without moving. The occasional boom of a shotgun or the spat of Adam's .22 signaled that the younger hunters were also finding targets.

I'd just stuffed the fifth squirrel, another black, into my game pocket when one of the shotguns spoke three times, fast. Seconds later the .22 cut loose, obviously emptying a thirty-shot clip. Yells followed, then several more shots. I hightailed it in that direction, joined quickly by Tommy and Mark. Adam and Deadeye appeared, talking excitedly.

"What happened?" Tommy yelled.

"Pack of wild dogs!" came the answer. "They came by Deadeye and he cut loose at them, then I emptied my rifle."

"How many?" Mark asked.

"I killed four and maybe crippled two more. Deadeye thinks he hit one. They went into the swamp. Must have been a dozen."

Over the years, we've had a real problem with wild dogs in this area. Town folks bring unwanted litters to the woods and turn them loose. I've seen packs of as many as thirty-five, and not only have my neighbors and I lost pets or livestock to them, but my daughter B.C. was mauled by one. After that, my rule has been to shoot the strays on sight.

Between us, we'd collected two dozen squirrels. Deadeye had killed another that hung in a crotch, and Adam had witnessed his futile attempt at retrieval.

"He was almost to it when he grabbed a dead limb that broke off. He came out of that tree head first, and I figured he was gonna break his neck. But at the last second he twisted and hit on his shoulder. Scared me to death!"

"You hurt yourself?" I asked.

"No, sir," was the laconic reply. "The ground was soft down there close to the swamp."

All hands turned to cleaning bushytails when we reached camp. The temperature had climbed into the upper thirties, and it was comfortable without a coat as long as we were busy. Mark and Tommy finished washing the cut-up pieces and packed them in an ice chest while Adam and Deadeye toasted up cheese sandwiches and I opened some soft drinks. I felt a little drowsy as I stretched out in front of the fire, but the youngsters obviously didn't. They were plotting against the rabbit population.

"Mark's got to work this afternoon, so I'll have to take him out anyway," Adam was saying. "And Blue John said he was coming in at noon. I'll pick up him and the Labradors while y'all break camp. Then we'll hunt that treeline and ditchbank in the North Newground." He turned to me. "You want to go, Daddy?"

"Nah, your mother wants me to watch the football game. But y'all go ahead."

Polar Bear, Windy, and Way bounded enthusiastically into the jeep at Adam's call when we returned to the house. Blue John was already there and swung into the seat Mark vacated.

"See you at school!" Adam yelled as the jeep backed out of the driveway. Mark grinned and waved.

"Had a good time!" he hollered at the departing hunters. Then, "Bye, Uncle Bob; I enjoyed it," he said to me as he headed to town to sack groceries for the rest of the afternoon.

I drowsed in front of the television for the next few hours, not really caring who won or lost. The boys trooped in not long after dark, muddy, tired, and happy. They'd killed eight big rabbits in the treeline, and the dogs had caught and retrieved two more. Blue John and Deadeye had walked into a covey of quail and downed four. Adam had added another as a lay bird flushed back over him. Tommy had bagged a woodcock, not too common an occurrence around here; he had thought it was

another quail. From a pothole in an adjoining beanfield, the boys had shot a half-dozen snipe, along with two late-season doves. One lone mallard had buzzed the same pothole just before sundown, and Blue John brought it down with a long shot. Since the Labs had already been sent home, Adam volunteered to drive around the field in the jeep and pick it up. He had chased the duck down, but then stuck the jeep on the way back. Since it had taken them an hour to get it out, Tommy had had to postpone his plans for the deer hunt.

The game had all been cleaned and washed, so Adam and Tommy packed it into plastic bags for the freezer. I watched with approval while Deadeye and Blue John cleaned and oiled all the guns, most of which stayed in my den. Betsy served fried venison steaks, rice and gravy, and hot buttered biscuits to the hunters, after making them wash their hands. It didn't seem at all strange to me that they'd taken such pains to clean both game and guns, but hadn't thought of washing up before eating. I had been a boy once, too.

Sometimes I wish I were again!

Adam

FROG FEVER, FROG MUSIC, AND DANCING FROGS

THE YOUNGSTER IN THE FRONT OF THE CANOE focused his headlight on the biggest bullfrog of the night, and saw there was going to be a real problem in getting to it. The croaker sat beneath an elbow bush at the edge of gig range, but the main trouble perched on a limb four feet above—a stumptail moccasin! Yet the boy rose to the challenge; this frog was too big to pass up.

"I'll lean way out to gig while you ease us in," he said to his companion running the outboard motor, "and you keep your light on that snake and holler if he starts to drop out of the bush." The kid in the middle seat nodded agreement.

The gigger pulled enough slack in the headlight cord to enable him to pose precariously across the bow of the old square-sterned Grumman canoe, holding himself in with feet and knees. His gig extended another eight feet from his long arms. "Ready," he signaled the driver.

The stumptail glowered at the trio as the canoe began inching under the elbow bush. "Just a little closer," muttered the forward lookout. Then, as he lunged to spear his victim, his companions saw the snake uncoil and drop from its perch.

The combination of a forceful forward lunge at the same moment as the nine-horse motor roared into full speed reverse produced results none of the frog hunters had witnessed before. The gigger lay face-down in four feet of water when his vehicle left him in the lurch, so to speak. And though lying on the water is often practiced, especially by fishermen, in this case it was only a temporary position. The remaining occupants of the canoe saw the gigged frog emerge from the depths well before the frog gigger, and it was months before they were able to convince their friend that the snake had actually left the branch at that particular moment.

Such are the perils of frog-gigging. Encounters with snakes are an intimate part of the sport. Only the taste of froglegs makes the collection of the same worthwhile.

Though the traditional view of frog hunting involves gigs, headlights, boats, snakes, and darkness, there are other ways to pursue the succulent amphibians. As a Mississippi Delta farm boy, one of my earliest hunting experiences was for frogs. Big Robert would perch me on the front fender of his pickup truck and drive around the ditches and sloughs on summer afternoons. From this vantage point, I could see bullfrogs sitting on the bank or in shallow water, and signal Daddy to stop when I had a clear shot. Using a .22 rifle, I would aim just behind the frog's head and fire, vaulting from the fender at the report. We ate froglegs a lot in those days.

A generation later, I watched the same type operation going on with the same driver, but a grandson instead of a son this time. Big Robert was recovering from an aneurysm that summer, and my son Adam was an enthusiastic nine-year-old frog hunter. Every afternoon the two of them, accompanied by Adam's young black Lab, Windy, would work the ditches, culverts, sloughs, and ponds on our place, as well as neighboring plantations. The result was not only a lot of prime eating, but a three-way friendship that I firmly believe led to a full recovery for Big Robert.

When shooting frogs, one must remember that, as with most cold-blooded living things, the nerve systems of frogs are long-lived. Use a bullet that will stop the victim in its tracks so that quick retrieval is possible. Hollow-point .22 long rifle cartridges seem to work best for us. Using solid-point bullets, in my opinion, will cripple many frogs that then escape to die a slow death. I have used .22 short hollow-points, but only in a pinch. The larger .22 magnums also work well, again in hollow-point.

Taking frogs in this manner also provides some challenging pistol shooting for those outdoorsmen who enjoy handguns, like Dude and Mountain Willy. (Willy brought over a pistol once that was so big I couldn't shoot it one-handed. Had a scope even.) Although I am not a bowhunter, I would think that frogging in this fashion also could provide an archer with fun, food, and practice during the off-season. Rarely are frog shots taken at more than twenty yards.

Perhaps those who have never taken frogs by the daytime drive-in method are beginning to believe their own legs are being pulled. "Why would a bullfrog sit still while someone in a pickup (or jeep, tractor, etc.) drives up and shoots them at less than twenty feet?" Well, there is a secret, of course.

Basically, it's all in the music.

Try an experiment of your own here: put down the book, get in your vehicle, and drive down to the nearest frog-bearing ditch. Approach the amphibian as closely as possible, then stop the engine, open the door, and step out. The frog will indeed dive beneath the waters before your door is all the way open.

Now, drive a ways farther, find an undisturbed frog, tune your radio to a good country or rock and roll station, adjust the volume to high, and advance upon your intended victim. It will sit there almost long enough for you to catch it bare-handed. Heavy metal, rap songs, classical music (excluding the William Tell and 1812 Overtures), and real mushy love songs don't seem to work nearly as well as country or rock and roll. Not enough holding power, obviously. Also, be warned that bullfrogs will often jump during commercials. Be ready when the song ends.

Actually, it's the noise that holds them (which is the same condition many teenagers wander around in these days). Whether it's music noise, engine noise (a tractor is better than a truck, unless the truck is mufflerless), or some other type of regular beat, the frogs will jump once the noise is shut down. Never cut the motor or radio off until after the shot is made.

One night Adam and I were paddling a ten-foot boat down a canal, having little luck gigging. The frogs seemed especially nervous, and we had no motor since we had carried our little boat over a quarter mile to the canal. From upstream we kept hearing a strange, somewhat familiar, high-pitched buzzing, and soon spied another light. The buzzing ceased when we flashed our headlight toward the newcomer, and soon he paddled up to us.

"Any luck?" I asked.

In answer, he opened an ice chest to reveal a squirming mess of good-sized frogs. Adam and I gawked in jealous admiration. "Well," I shook my head, "we haven't done much so far. They seem to be kinda skittish on this end of the canal."

The stranger grinned. "You haven't waked 'em up yet, have you?" He leaned forward and shone his beam on the middle seat of his john boat. There sat the source of the weird buzzing we had heard. It was a regular old run-of-the-mill windup alarm clock.

"They're usually skittish unless you wake 'em up," we were instructed, and the pro touched his cap bill politely while he paddled past us two amateurs. As he rounded a bend and went out of sight, we heard the buzzing begin again. The next thing we heard faintly was the sound of his icebox lid slamming shut on yet another "waked-up" bullfrog.

No pun intended, but he wasn't alarming the frogs.

Day or night hunting, shooting, gigging, or grabbing, some regular noise seems to lull the frogs into a false sense of security. If the frogs are skittish, and you don't have a motor operating, try an alarm clock or radio. With all due respect to the band Three Dog Night, the song that starts out about a bullfrog named Jeramiah should work quite appropriately.

When hunting frogs at night gigging is, of course the traditional method of taking the prey. A sharp, three-pronged gig mounted on a stout handle is a must when gigging off muddy banks, so common in the Delta. The soft mud will cushion the gig thrust enough that the frog will often be simply mashed into the bank with a dull gig or a limber pole. An old cotton-chopping hoe provides a good stout handle, though not quite as long as most frog hunters prefer. In case of a snake attack, a five-foot gig leaves very little room for the gigger when it is used to impale a five-foot cottonmouth.

One gig in the boat is enough, too. There was a case recently when three friends went gigging in the nearby "bar pits" with a long and a short gig. Somehow, in the midst of all the action, the short gig ended up in the thigh of one of the hunters. The trio was able to clip the shanks off the gig points, and remove all but one of the barbs from the unfortunate victim, but that last one was impaled too deeply for amateurs. A trip to the emergency room of a nearby hospital was indicated.

The intern on duty there was a foreign medical student from the East, who not only had never been frog gigging, but spoke broken English to compound the problem. To make matters worse, the victim was a native Australian who had come to the United States for his education just like the doctor. Further verbal complications were caused by the fact that the only available painkiller during removal of the first two barbs was the standard bottle of bourbon so familiar to western movie fans, which is always produced for arrow removal after the Indian attack on the wagon train. Let's just say that there was a language barrier.

Finally, one of the hunters procured paper and pen from the nurse at the reception desk, and drew a picture of a frog gig, with a close-up of the double-barbed point in the Australian's leg. An international understanding was reached, and removal of the offending shank was effected. Thereafter, the leader of the gigging party was heard to brag that they had bagged "fourteen frogs and an Aussie!"

One of my oft-time gigging companions nearly lost an arm after a frogging expedition one night. Joe had been cleaning his catch one morning, and his knife slipped, cutting him slightly across one knuckle. He didn't think too much of the nick, finished his frog-cleaning, washed his hands, and applied a Band-Aid. That night, the two of us took our wives out to supper and a picture show.

While we were standing in line to buy tickets, Joe complained that his hand was hurting. Inside, at the popcorn counter, we noticed that little red streaks were visible on his wrist. Halfway through the show, he excused himself to go to the restroom, and returned to roust me out of my seat. In the lobby lights, I could see that the red streaks were up past his elbow, and he was obviously in pain. I went to get the girls, and we headed for the hospital.

The red steaks were almost to the shoulder when the doctor examined Joe and diagnosed blood poisoning. "Frog Fever," he proclaimed, after we had explained where the infection had probably come from. We left the hospital a couple of hours later with a groggy ex-gigger, shot up with antibiotics and other drugs, his hand wrapped in gauze to the size of a boxing glove and encased in a sterile plastic bag to contain an extremely virulent infection. The doctor, who is an old hunting buddy, has never forgotten "Joe's Frog Fever." Joe himself, if you can talk him into frog-gigging with you, will make you clean all the frogs.

Cleaning the frogs is a cinch with the right equipment. I like to include in the gear for a gigging expedition a pair of short powerful garden clippers. When a frog is taken, whether by shooting, gigging, or grabbing, it is simple to clip the backbone in two just above the pelvis, and flip the legs into the ice chest. After the hunt is over, it only takes a few moments to skin out the legs, not to mention the fact that an ice chest holds more legs than whole frogs.

Plenty of ice in the ice chest, one gig in the boat, the hedge clippers, headlight, spotlight, alarm clock or radio, snakebite kit, and painkiller: these are the essentials for a quality frog-gigging trip. However, one doesn't always need a gig or a gun to successfully gather bullfrogs. When I was in high school, Troy and I used to keep the science teacher supplied with dissection frogs for his biology labs. Mr. Edwards paid two bits a frog, but the frog had to be unpunctured; in perfect health. Therefore, Troy and I learned to grab the amphibians. Same techniques, just reaching out with our hands and snaring the critters. The main disagreement I have with this method, is that it places the grabber about six feet closer to the snakes which are on the banks right along with the bullfrogs.

But it kept us in dating money back in those times when a boy and girl could go to a drive-in movie with popcorn, hot dogs, and R-O-Cs for less than five bucks. I might add that this arrangement ended when Troy and I held out one especially lively frog one morning to place in Miss Smith's drawer in senior girls homeroom. It produced quite

a show, but Mr. Edwards was able to add two and two, unfortunately for us grabbers.

One can learn several biology lessons from frogs, by the way; and not just in laboratory surroundings. One night I was out frog-gigging with Adam and a friend of his when they were young. We were wading, with headlights, in a shallow pond not too far from the house, when suddenly I heard one of the boys exclaim to the other, "Look! What are those frogs doing?"

I shone my light over toward them, and spied a pair of large frogs, one atop the other. They squirmed together as the boys watched in fascination. "Gig 'em!" I urged, knowing I was going to have to come up with an explanation, and not wanting this to get any more complicated than necessary. Mark complied, and it's the only time in my life that I ever saw two frogs gigged at one stab.

"What were they doing, Daddy?" Adam asked the inevitable question.

As both boys waited wide-eyed for my answer, I was inspired by the strains coming from the nearby jeep. We had left the radio on, so as to mask our wading noise and lull the frogs. I disremember the tune that was playing, but it made the answer obvious.

"Why, dancing, son. Those were dancing frogs!"

THE WILD HARES OF YOUTH

THE YOUNGSTER WE HAD PLACED AT THE JUNCTION of the North Newground ditch and the Little Canal was getting antsy, I could tell. From the canal bend where I was stationed, less than a hundred yards from Sanfrid, I could see him switching nervously from side to side, pointing his twenty-gauge first at the clear spot on the ditch shaded by the big oak, then back toward the burnt-off clearing along the canal. His agitation increased as the baying of the hounds drew closer and closer to us.

Suddenly, he swung and fired twice at the canal bank, took two running steps in that direction, then just as suddenly braked and shouldered the shotgun again, this time aiming back to his left on the ditch. From my vantage point, I could see a fast-moving brown streak cross in front of the oak, then Sanfrid's twenty boomed again. The rabbit flipped, and the kid reached in his pocket for more shells. I was just fixing to send a cheer his way when two more cottontails burst from the junction of ditch and canal, and raced directly for the boy. As he fumbled frantically to reload, the beagles, in full cry, broke cover right behind the rabbits making a beeline for the cover of the soybean field. Sanfrid bellowed a wild war cry as the bunnies bounded to either side of him and his empty gun, his cry quickly drowned out by the pack of equally bellowing beagles swirling around him. Miss Adventure actually ran between the youngster's legs!

Rabbit hunting action in the Mississippi Delta can be fast and furious, especially if you have access to a good pack of those little beagles, and a few kids.

On another hunt with this same youngster in this same North Newground, I saw him charged by seven rabbits at once, when they broke cover in flight from their pursuers. To his credit, he did get three of the seven, but he was so shaken he couldn't reload.

This type of action is not particularly uncommon in the Delta farming country at the right time. In the fall, when the fields are being harvested, the rabbits have to move their housekeeping operations to the ditchbanks and old fencelines, and these fieldside coverts will be literally teeming with cottontails for a few weeks. Until the ubiquitous coyotes have thinned out the population. If hunters can move into action during this critical period, they'll have some wild times, and beagles fit right into the picture with the youngsters.

My family has been in the beagle business for years; some of my earliest memories are of Nip and Tuck in full cry after the yard rabbit. Forty years later, as I write this, I can hear Josephine's high-pitched bay as she chases what is probably a descendent of that same yard rabbit around the same pasture, accompanied by our yellow Lab, Lexy.

When one lives in the country, a couple of good loud beagles and a Lab that looks big enough for a capable bite (whether they bite or not) are about the best burglary insurance policies money can buy. That's one real good reason for keeping beagles at country homes. Yet, one of my neighbors clings steadfastly to the opinion that a flock of guinea fowl are better noisemakers than my beagles, and have the advantage of egg-laying. While I'll concede that the beagles I've owned have never laid eggs, it's my own observation that guinea fowl won't run rabbits. Both of us will agree, however, that a pack of beagles in pursuit of a flock of guineas produces a cacophony worthy of some kind of award! And I've had some real award-winning beagles in my time.

My biggest and best pack of beagles came from an unplanned brother and sister union. Belle got romantic while I was busy planting cotton one year, and Trigger was the proud father, and uncle, of a whole six-pack of pups. While such a sibling mating can result in all kind of genetic setbacks, sometimes it goes the other way, and you get all the good traits. That fall I took the whole kit and kaboodle down to the woods in the jeep, and durned if I didn't more or less park right on top of a big old swamp rabbit. The pups piled out of the vehicle into a dewberry patch, and the canecutter bowled little Thirteen right over in his bid for escape. When I stepped around the jeep to see what all the commotion was about, that rabbit was busting out of the patch with Eric the Red literally hanging onto his tail, and Sam, Seven, Beaudine, and Miss Adventure in hot pursuit, while Thirteen scrambled to regain her feet. That was all the training that young pack ever needed.

Often, a good pack of dogs will actually train their own hunters, strange as that sounds. When I was a kid, we had a mixed pack of rabbit runners that included the hounds Soupie and Jupiter Pluvius, the huge golden Labrador Yank, and Freckles, the pointer. Why that bird dog never pointed or chased rabbits on bird hunts was always a mystery to me, since he was an expert at rabbit-running when on his own time. This group would sometimes consent to my joining them for an expedition. Jupiter and Soupie would go to the other end of the ditchbank and begin their melodious push back our way, while Yank and Freckles would station themselves at the end of the ditch, with me in the middle. Everyone had their own territory, that was obvious.

As the hounds got closer and closer, I could hear some telltale rustles in the weeds, and sure enough, soon the bunnies would begin popping out in escape attempts that were all too often futile. I'd usually be armed with a little Marlin .22 carbine, shooting short hollow-points. Yank and Freckles needed only their teeth. The really strange thing was that even though one of the dogs might catch and quickly kill a canecutter on his side, no one ever ate a bite until the hounds had completed the drive. Then they'd all share in the meal. I swear it. I was allowed to carry my own kill home, but at that tender age, there was no way I was going to try to claim one of theirs. I always got the impression that I was simply tolerated because they considered me one of Big Robert and Miss Janice's pups!

As a youngster myself, I broke in hunting on these same ditchbanks and canals after rabbits. There were a lot of sharecroppers on the Delta plantations back then, and after the crops were harvested, hunting parties gathered on most clear days. Even the "pot-likker" hounds would run rabbits, and cotton tail cover was more plentiful in cotton country in the old days. As many as a dozen men and boys with their dogs, would work the thickets, sloughs, ditchbanks, and canals, often on all-day hunts. That's when having small dogs came in handy. Not only could the little hounds negotiate the dense canebrakes and briar patches better, but when they tired at the end on the day, a game vest was a comfortable fit for a ride home. Many's the time I returned from a hunt with a limit of rabbits strung from my belt and a beagle nestled in the vest on my back.

As was the case with the pup Eric the Red, sometimes the small beagles bite off more than they can chew with the big swamp rabbits common to the Delta. Adam and I were once positioned atop the canal bank, right down from where the bunnies and beagles charged Sanfrid that day, while Belle, Angel, and Trigger pushed toward us. As they neared, Trigger broke cover on the field side, made a short loop on a cold trail into the beans, and re-entered the johnson grass right below us. In the meantime, Angel jumped the rabbit she was trailing, down next to the water. The panicked canecutter turned straight up the bank, and broke cover almost at our feet, just as Trigger topped the rise from the opposite way. They met head-on, and just from reflex the dog opened his mouth, whether to bay or bite, I never knew. Whatever he intended, he got a gracious mouthful of fleeing swamp rabbit, headed in the direction from whence he had come. Neither Adam nor I could shoot, of course, as the miniature hound was rudely jerked back over the bank and the two tumbled head over heels into the grass patch with Angel and Belle right behind in full cry. After the canecutter made his escape, Trigger reappeared with the most embarrassed expression on his face. "Boy! He's lucky he got away!" the little beagle seemed to say to us.

Adam used to have a black Lab named Windy, and the two of them had an unusual arrangement for rabbit hunting. Windy was named for her speed, and caught many a cottontail on her own. It was not uncommon at all during those years for Adam to leave the house after school for a short hunt, shoot a couple of times, and come in with four or five rabbits an hour later. Not only would Windy retrieve the ones he shot, but she'd usually bring in just as many as her young master did, all by herself!

Our family has always been just as involved in raising Labradors as beagles. The two breeds work well together; we don't keep male Labs, and the enthusiastic (but too short!) little male beagles are sure indicators when one of the lady Labs begins her romantic cycle. One year we kept a couple of Windy's pups (kids and pups form attachments at times that are impossible to break; if we had sold black Wayward Wind or yellow-white Polar Bear, we'd have had to sell Adam, Christie, and B.C.!) who grew to be nearly as fast as their mother. Now that was a rabbit-hunting combination!

Young Tommy Hendrix once borrowed those three Labs for a short hunt and soon returned, disgusted, with seven canecutters, never having even fired a shot. "They take all the fun out of it," he complained. "It's almost like they just took *me* hunting with *them* so I could carry back their rabbits!" The dogs would surround a briar or weed patch, Polar Bear would take a flying leap into the middle, and the Windy & Way Team would go into action, quickly chasing down, then retrieving, the flushed cottontails.

The only disadvantage with using the Labs is that none of them will bark except at potential burglars or a coyote pack at three in the morning. We often solve that problem by hunting the two breeds together, like Lexy and Josephine are doing even as I write. Seldom do we ever pen our dogs up (except for romance purposes), so they all get a lot of practice on the yard rabbits.

If one doesn't own a do-it-themselves dog pack, bagging the bunnies demands a weapon of some type, usually a shotgun. In the thickets, briarpatches, and canebrakes of the Delta, rifles are generally frowned upon, although they are legal. Too much chance of a ricochet or stray bullet going further than intended. It's also a good idea to clothe the hunters in orange, red, yellow, or some other highly visible color. Since camouflage is not needed on a rabbit hunt, and snap-shots are the rule rather than the exception, safety is a prime consideration. The .410 or twenty gauge is enough gun for most hunters, and that's another reason rabbit hunting is such a great way to introduce a youngster to the joys of being afield.

In my own youth, I could not help but be impressed at the favorite weapon of one of our sharecroppers who often hunted with us. Robert Moses used a "tapstick" he made himself by drilling one end of a cut-off hoe handle and weighting it with lead. About eighteen inches long, the tapstick was deadly in the hands of an accurate thrower. Robert could hit with it nearly every time inside of twenty yards, especially if the rabbit was momentarily stopped, as they often do. Anyone within fifty yards could hear his grunt of concentration when he threw, much like a pitcher releasing a fast ball.

Another tapstick hunter, Longmile Harrison, was the one who showed me the proper way to carry rabbits. He'd cut through the skin behind the hamstring tendon and string the bunnies on his belt by the hind legs. It's a lot less back-breaking than packing half-a-dozen canecutters that may weigh as much as eight pounds each in one's game vest. Of course, Longmile also wore suspenders to keep his britches up.

It was a modern-day companion, the famous Dude McElwee, who taught Adam and me how to lighten the load even more, by "slinging" the rabbits we bagged. It's a useful and interesting field-dressing method that also, in my opinion, insures that the meat will be even better than usual—and that's the best part of rabbit hunting.

Dude holds the cottontail head-up, gripping it firmly just below the rib cage. Squeezing tightly, he then moves his hands slowly downward, "milking" the guts toward the tail. Rabbits are notoriously thin-skinned, as every hunter knows, and the entrails so forced down will break out between the hind legs. When they do, Dude just "slings" the insides right out of the rabbit, never even getting his hands bloody. Lightens the load, insures the taste, and makes cleaning easier when the day is done. Try it.

Speaking of taste, rabbit is better table fare than any game except quail and wild turkey, in my opinion. Adam and his young companions had a standing seasonal request for once-a-week fried rabbit, with rice and gravy. Soak the meat in milk before deep-fat frying, and it's better than the standard Southern fried chicken, hands down. But I've discovered an even better way, by accident.

Betsy had planned a supper of shish-ka-bob duck, which is one of my grill specialties. She got a package of what appeared to be duck from the freezer and dropped it in Italian Dressing to thaw and marinate. That evening, though, I found that the package had actually been rabbit. Since my fire was already going on the grill, I decided to try shish-ka-bob bunny, and now we rarely eat it any other way. Fillet the meat from the loins and hindquarters; skewer it with pineapple chunks, peppers, mushrooms, cherry tomatoes, and onions; and grill it over fairly hot coals, turning and basting frequently. Use the marinade for a sauce base, adding Worchestershire and a jar of mint jelly to taste as they simmer and blend. It'll make you hurt yourself!

Back during the turnrow-to-turnrow farming era of the seventies and early eighties, rabbit habitat got rather scarce in the Delta. The influx and build-up of the coyote population was also a negative factor for rabbit hunters. However, the introduction of the Conservation Reserve Program has produced a great deal of game habitat during the past five years, and no longer do beagle owners have to go far afield to find enough range for their hounds. Be sure to ask permission from the landowner before releasing your dogs, however. Many farmers are like myself: they have a pack of beagles and Labs, a young son and his companions, and a hankering for shish-ka-bob bunny!

OPENING DAY DELTA DOVES

THE LONE DOVE WINGING SWIFTLY DOWN THE center of Frank Tindall's harvested cornfield was really way too high, especially for a kid with a twenty gauge double-barrel on his first hunt. But I was too young and inexperienced to know that. Manfully, I swung the little gun with the sawed-off stock to my shoulder, plugged in a sizable (if ignorant) lead, and fired away!

Blind hogs sometimes find acorns, it is said.

The dove went straight up, headshot. Finally, just before it seemed that it would fly right into the sun, it set its wings in a long death glide. Once more, the gray darter's course took it down the center of the field, but this time there was a difference.

Now it was *my* dove; my first dove—the first I had ever shot at! I breeched the double barrel, laid it on my vest, and took off down the length of my Godfather's disked cornfield, determined that this particular dove was not going to get away. The glide must have lasted at least a hundred yards, but I was right there when *my* dove hit the ground. I was all by myself when I picked up the beautiful little gray bird—or so I thought. Suddenly, I realized that the whole field was cheering! For me!

I remember being struck speechless when I killed my first buck; my first gobbler left me with the shakes for half a day; my first duck was *not* going to lie out there in that dirty water any longer than necessary—Big Robert had to paddle across Swan Lake for it before I'd let him shoot again. But nothing compares to the pride of holding one's first dove in a crowded field while those giants who raised him cheer his accomplishment. Mi'ter Mo' was the closest to me, but after he shook my hand, I had to run the gamut of Uncle Shag, Big John, Frank, Mr. Gardner, Uncle Sam, and Big Dave, that I remember. My hand was nearly too sore to hold the gun, after all that congratulatory shaking!

And honestly, I couldn't tell you if I killed another dove or not that day. But I'll never forget that first one, forty years ago! And now I was experiencing some deja vu.

A few days before, a policeman from a nearby town called to ask permission to bring his boy out to the farm for Opening Day. "He's never hunted before, but he knows how to handle a gun, and I'll keep him close to me," he assured me. Of course, I was quick to grant permission, and they were crouched in the edge of the field just down from B.C. and myself. A drifter swept out of the bordering cotton field right over the youngster's head, and reflexes took over. The bird literally exploded into a cloud of feathers at the boy's shot.

And the kid got the shakes.

Teeth chattering, he turned to me and exclaimed, "T-that's my f-first d-dove!" I didn't need to be told; I was watching the father as he strode to retrieve the bird. In ten short steps, the man's chest had grown from a size forty to a forty-six! Pride may be one of the Seven Deadly Sins, but I'll bet the Good Lord forgives it in cases like this. I wouldn't give a plugged nickel for a father who didn't take some pride in his kid's first dove.

Later, over a cold drink, the policeman waxed philosophic: "More fathers ought to take the time to teach their kids to hunt. A lot of the problems we see in my line of work might could be headed off if parents spent more quality time outdoors with their youngsters."

I tend to agree. I was doing the same thing with my own daughter. And not five minutes after the cop's boy pasted his first dove, B.C. scored too, dropping one from a crossing flock.

My Sweet Sixteen was very nonchalant about having made a really good shot on the speeding bird, causing the watching policeman's son to ask jealously, "How long has she been hunting?"

B.C. downed the bird with a little twenty-gauge pump that had been her grandfather's. She considers that pumpgun as her very own, just as my son claimed the old sixteen-gauge pump from the same grandfather. The year that Adam was twelve, he picked up forty-five doves out of three boxes of shells during the three-day Opening Weekend on Labor Day. Since that showing many years ago, the Model twelve Winchester has been his favorite gun for doves.

Only a couple of years after that experience, Adam was shooting that same shotgun the Opening Day that I put him, Bobby Baird, and Bobby's son, Bill, out of my pickup next to the cottonwood tree in the millet field. I continued down the field letting other hunters out, then returned for another load. But when I passed the cottonwood, Bobby was right there waiting for me,

119

even though he had only been in the field maybe fifteen minutes.

"You got a limit already?" I asked, slightly incredulous.

"Heck, naw!" my friend replied. "But take me somewhere else. That boy of yours has hit ten straight shots, and I'm not fixing to shoot next to someone that good. Put me by some normal shooter."

Couple of years later, Bobby got his revenge. I was shooting next to Bill the Opening Day that youngster couldn't miss. Several of us moved away that afternoon!

*   *   *   *   *   *   *   *   *   *   *

B.C. followed up her good shot by missing twice on a pair of doves loafing by against the breeze, easy right-to-lefters. Beau was next in line, and as usual he pulled a classy double, wiping B.C.'s eye. His son Will, an enthusiastic seven-year-old, charged out of the soybean rows to retrieve the pair. Will would probably be big enough to shoot next year, but I was willing to bet that he'd never put on an Opening Day exhibition as spectacular as the one Beau once performed.

*   *   *   *   *   *   *   *   *   *   *

When he was a senior in high school, my younger brother had taught us all a new lesson about dedication to hunting. He had broken his right collarbone in a football collision, and was released from the hospital in a cast only a week before dove season. Beau went straight to the gun cabinet for a .22 rifle and shells, and for the next week shot several hundred rounds a day from his left shoulder. On Saturday, Opening Day, he took his twenty gauge out and shot fifty percent—from the left side!

* * * * * * * * * * *

Across the newly-planted wheat field from us, the report of a shotgun was accompanied by a huge cloud of smoke. Ronny James, an old college roommate and fraternity brother, was using a muzzle-loading shotgun this year. That cloud reminded me of the second year Ronny had come down to the Brownspur hunt, back in the early sixties.

* * * * * * * * * * *

Three of us Ole Miss Pikes had decided to go together to try to save some bucks on shells that year. Herndon, Ronny, and I pooled our money and bought enough reloading supplies to last most of dove season, but then Herndon fell in love before the actual reloading took place. With little time to spare from romance, he asked Ronny and me to just reload his third of the shells. We obliged.

By careful experimentation, we found that a certain mixture of sand and confetti would approximate the weight of number eight shot. We went to great pains to use this mixture instead of shot in about one-fourth of Herndon's shells. Of course, it took a little extra time, but what's a little time to True Brothers of the Bond?

That Opening Day, Herndon had one of the hottest spots in the field, right by the fork in the pond. After his initial volleys revealed our prank, he spread his shells out on the ground and

attempted to separate them by weight—to no avail. Outside of using an X-ray, his only recourse seemed to be just shooting up the shells, and in no time at all, the ground around his stand resembled an early snowfall. If his first shot was confetti, Herndon couldn't see through the white cloud for a second shot at the speeding dove. Yet, if the first shell was okay, he was so rattled that his lead would be off. Hunters came all the way across the twenty-five-acre field to witness the action, except for me and Ronny; we stayed at a safe distance. We also spent the rest of the semester fearful of Herndon's revenge—but that's another story!

*   *   *   *   *   *   *   *   *   *   *

The worst thing about Opening Day is that these embarrassing incidents are always in front of fifty to a hundred other hunters. Therefore, one is never allowed to forget them. For instance, the Old Dove Season Bunch will always remember the sight of an eighty-pound southbound golden Labrador, intent on retrieving his first dove, hitting the end of the leash attached to his master's ankle, just as said master was swinging on the second dove, now northbound, intent on making the first double of Opening Day.

One younger hunter really got broken in poorly, simply because he took the Dove Season Bunch too seriously. Probably a dozen of us were sitting out behind Beau's house, picking doves, the year of Pat's first hunt. Seems there was a pretty liberal limit back then, maybe eighteen, and we had all limited out. Then Big Robert drove up with Uncle Sam, Uncle Shag, Big Dave, Mi'ter Mo', Mister Hurry, Mister Hally, Mister Tut, and a couple of others we respected as our elders. "You kids clean our doves, too, while we go wash up for the Party," was the universal order. They emptied their game bags into our pile. There must have been 400 doves mounded inside the circle of us pickers.

An hour later a dark green pickup pulled into the driveway.

Game wardens often drive such vehicles down here in our part of the country, so that's the first thought we all had. And there we sat with at least two limits apiece for each picker present. "Oh, my Lord," Pat exclaimed. "What are we gonna do if he comes back here?"

With a sideways wink at the rest of us, Gary reached over for his shotgun, pumped a shell into the chamber, laid it across his lap, and picked up another dove. "Well, I reckon we'll just have to kill the son of a bitch," he declared matter-of-factly.

Pat never said a word. He rose, spun, walked to the fence, crossed same, and disappeared into the trees, headed for Big Robert's house, across the pasture. I don't remember him hunting with us again.

Other memorable Opening Day events we will never forget are the year a cropduster crashed into the field—and the pilot walked away unhurt! Hard to top that year. Then there was the time that Fred volunteered to be checked by the game warden, only to find that the gunsmith had neglected to replace the plug in his gun after repairing it. Or the time that Dude "mooned" at Fred for a good-natured insult, and it turned out there was a lady hunter in the field, at close range. That one generated a Mooning Turkey Award at the Opening Day Party that evening!

The Party is almost like New Year's for most of us; we have hunted together for years, some of us since grammar school. That evening is planned for months in advance, and for some of the crowd, it's the one time of year they see everybody else. Actually, if we were to take a poll, we would probably find that most of us plan on the Party more than the Hunt! Semmes Ross, now hunting just down from us with his son Alan, and I used to sing together in our fraternity quartet at Ole Miss. No one in our crowd would ever let us forget the 1969 Opening Day Party after we returned home from the service. We were belting out "The Impossible Dream" in harmony while Betsy and Ann Dye accompanied us on the piano. Before we finished the second verse, the police called to say we were disturbing the neighbors. Of course, it *was* two in the morning! That was a good Party!

Time flies when you're having fun; on Opening Day three years ago, Alan Ross had picked up his own first dove. And young Daniel Dye, son of another college fraternity brother and roomie, had gotten his first the year before, the day of the plane crash. Gary (married to our late-night pianist) and I had been the second ones to reach the wreck, in my pickup. The first ones had been Adam's group of fifteen-year-olds, in the jeep. That was the year that Beau and I had turned over the job of driving around the field with ice water and colas to the next generation. What a momentous event by which to remember their coming-of-age Opening Day! That crash had earned the unhurt pilot an invitation to the hunt and Party the following year. We crowned David with one of those beanies with a propeller on top (which my oldest daughter, Christie, had searched all over New Orleans for,

between her classes at Tulane) and presented him
with a special award in verse, one stanza of which
went :

And now the plane is upside down,
And now it's rightside up!
And now it's flying toward the ground,
And now it's bouncing up!
Oh, David, Daring David; hold on to your seat!
For Opening Day Action, this show can't be
beat!
The epic poem closed with:
Oh, David, Daring David! We honor your
survival.
The high point of our hunt last year,
Was your Opening Day Arrival!

Last season, David's son Lloyd proudly
showed me his first dove, bagged on Opening Day
in a field right across the road from where his
father had earned the Flying Turkey Award.

There have been literally hundreds of younger
hunters who have broken in on our Opening Day
hunts over the forty-some-odd years it has been
held. We are into our fourth generation, in some
cases. And not all the kids have been bred-in-the-
bone, so to speak. Several years ago, Christie
invited a friend from Tulane to come up for
Opening Day. Robert was a city boy, and had
never hunted anything at all. He was an immediate favorite, though, and Adam took him under his
wing, though Robert was probably six years older.
After careful instruction, my son placed the boy
right down the fence from himself, so he could
coach if needed. The need was certainly there.
One of Robert's first shots was at a bird at least

150 yards away. Nearly everyone in the field heard his yelled question after the dove kept on flying: "Will this thing shoot that far?" To his credit, Adam did make a hunter out of the kid, who still comes back for Opening Day.

This past year, I looked around the Opening Day field, and couldn't help commenting on the fact that over half of the hunters were under twenty. Remember that old saying we've all heard before? "What goes around, comes around!" Beau was quick to remind me that there had come a time during our growing up years, when Big Robert and Uncle Sam had commented on the same phenomenon. Matter of fact, their exact words were: "Why don't y'all give the Party next Opening Day? There's more young folks than older ones here!" Now I'm almost there myself.

Yet I believe this generation of kids is ready to accept the gavel. Only a couple of years before, I had been watching an older hunter who had developed an arthritic hip, and was having trouble making shots to his left. Adam drifted in soon, having limited out, and pulled a cold drink from the ice chest. He popped the cap, sipped the R-O-C, and struck up a conversation with Dr. Chollie, who had roomed with Big Robert in college. As they talked, the youngster's eyes strayed to Mr. Flanagan and his obvious problems, which also included walking to retrieve his doves. Finishing his drink, the boy excused himself and walked over to Mr. Flanagan's side. He spent the rest of the afternoon retrieving the older hunter's doves, and warning him in plenty of time for shots coming from the left.

No, I'm not bragging because he's mine; there are another dozen kids the same age whom I have seen doing almost the same thing. Bryon McIntire volunteered to drive the jeep with the cold drinks at last year's Opening Day, and Tommy Burford offered for he and Mark to clean the doves Dude and I had managed to collect. That whole bunch of "Jakes" helped prepare the field, and cooked much of the food for the Party. Joe and Deadeye cleaned up afterward, while Clif and Adam packaged doves for the freezer.

"Dadblame, we've done a good job with these kids!" I exclaimed to Gary, Dude, and Mountain Willy, who were relaxing on the patio with me, recalling past Opening Day hunts and Parties. They agreed.

It's time to pass Opening Day along to the next generation, once again. Good luck, youngsters. Carry on, while your elders supervise in rockers on the porch.

"Pour me another sip of that frog juice, Mountain Willy, and I'll tell y'all about the time that me and Big Robert took the .410s out Opening Day, on a bet. Those doves were coming in like sofa pillows, and we really put on a show, like Mr. June Cuming used to do when I was a kid. I hit...."

Mr. Hurry

"Mr. Hally"

David

GREAT AND NOT-SO-GREAT OUTDOOR MEDICAL MOMENTS

WHY IS IT THAT SOME PEOPLE HAVE GOOD LUCK and some have bad? I used to have a pastor who maintained that there was no such thing as luck; yet, after he had been around me for a while, Mike quit preaching that doctrine in public. During one afternoon in a fishing boat, he advised me that some guardian angels might be just a little bit more on the ball than mine obviously was, and promised to take the matter up in his next extended prayer period. He later moved, so I'm not sure what the final ruling was.

Momma used to say I could just walk through the room, and pictures would fall off the walls.

Now you take stinging insects, for instance. I went to disk up the garden one fall day and had Adam walk through it carefully to check for hoses, sprinklers, and such like that might still be around. After he gave me the all-clear signal, I put the tractor in gear and lowered the disk. On my second pass, I hit a nest of ground bumblebees, who immediately perceived that I was responsible for the destruction of their home and demanded vengeance. In my wild flight, I disked up hose, sprinkler, half a stacked cord of firewood, and an expensive pair of sunglasses that I knocked off my head swatting at the bees.

Why didn't they sting Adam when he walked by the nest? Matter of fact, they didn't even bother Betsy when she went back through a few minutes later to see if she could find the glasses. It's happened all my life; many times Big Robert, Beau, and I would be standing together and a malicious wasp would come cruising by, looking for a victim. Who always got selected? Me.

It's my cross to bear, I reckon. But it sure has kept our home-town physicians busy, all the way back to Doctor Bunt!

The medical fraternity takes a lot of flack, much of it undeserved. After reading a typical bitchy commentary not long ago, I got to thinking about the demands placed on doctors by at least this one outdoorsman.

Football. Was there ever a sport that required more medical attention, up to and including the Crusades? Just on this one body (that admittedly sounds like a bowl of Rice Krispies—"snap, crackle, pop"—when it gets out of bed in the mornings), physicians have been able, solely because of football, to practice their art on a broken wrist, thumb, and rib; to repair a shoulder and a hip joint; to heal a ruptured artery and a gangrenous leg; and to observe the effects of several concussions. Only two of these occurred during office hours; in fact, they probably averaged out around suppertime, since two others required attention close to midnight.

Nor does football's medical demand extend only to physicians. Twice I have seen dentists rousted out after dark to make emergency repairs on broken teeth—one of them mine. And as I remember it, there was an after-game job on a tackle that required both a doctor and a dentist; in addition to breaking a tooth, he had bitten through his tongue. Tackles are like that.

I don't think I ever played in a football game, junior high through college, when a doctor was not present, and as far as I have been able to ascertain, not a one of them was ever paid for being on the field with the team, until I reached the college level. The exception to that rule would be the school insurance payment when a kid was hurt. And some of us were obviously high-risk cases with large deductibles.

Other team-sport injuries, again using only personal experience, have included cartilage and

ligament damages to a foot and a knee, the latter being repeated many times, requiring at least one Sunday visit and finally a complete reconstruction of the knee. For ten years it seems like once each turkey season I'd have to get Doctor Carl to run that long needle up behind my kneecap and suck the bloody fluid off so the swelling would go down and I could hunt the next weekend.

Outdoor-related injuries have also served to keep my family doctors on their toes. After eleven o'clock on a Saturday night, Dr. John took a rusty trotline hook out of a bloody chunk of palm, fitted the ripped-out flesh back where it looked best, and put about a dozen stitches in it. Nearly three years later, at the same time of night, that hand again came under scrutiny as a result of being crushed in a cotton gin accident. Though freshly roused from a warm bed, Doctor Carl good-humoredly pointed out the fine stitchery to Nurse Ann. Once started on that train of thought, he drolly related tales of some of the nearly 100 stitches he and other local physicians had put me back together with over the years. The two of them had a fun midnight chat.

Weekends and Wednesday afternoons are the usual free time for doctors, but over the years I would guess that less than ten percent of my accidents have been during office hours. I get snakebit on Saturday or have jeep wrecks on Sundays and Wednesday afternoons. On the occasion when I broke four vertebrae, tore the cartilage away from my rib cage, and partially collapsed both lungs, Doctor Carl was already past the city limits headed for the lake when he heard the wail of the ambulance. He later told me, "I started to keep going, but then I thought, hell, since it's after hours, it's probably Neill and it's probably serious."

This trait obviously has some genetic basis, for it shows up to an extent in the next generation. When Adam was an infant, Betsy came down with a fast-moving birth-related infection and that night her temperature soared to 105. In a panic, I called and Doctor Carl came. He quickly diagnosed the problem, and said, "We don't have time to take her to a hospital. Make me some coffee, boy!" She was out of danger when he left at three a.m. I had matched cups of coffee with him and didn't sleep for a whole week. Never asked him how he did.

One Sunday afternoon a dozen years later, this same doctor sewed up this same boy's hand after a duck hunting accident in flooded woods. Who else would have a kid who could run up on a busted headlight floating in waist-deep water?

He also had an accident one summer while cutting wood and showed up at the house with a black eye, a lump the size of an egg, and enough flowing blood to slake a vampire's thirst for a week. After the (same) doctor had stitched him up (on the weekend!), Adam declared that it was all my fault. "Doctor Carl said I was just like my daddy," he glared.

This may not be entirely accurate, but then again, he may have a point. Even as I type this, the kid is laid up from the same type of knee ligament reconstruction operation that I had ten years ago. It even works long distance and by association. I was over in South Carolina fishing for bream with a friend, and he made reference to a chapter in one of my books about hooking oneself while fishing. As we floated parallel to the bank in the canoe, The Big C cast and remarked, "You know, in thirty-five years of fishing, I've never hooked myself."

He shouldn't have said it.

Not fifteen minutes later, a small voice from the back of the canoe said, "Could you come help me for a minute?"

You guessed it. His popping bug hook had sunk into the ball of his thumb up to the barb. He had grabbed it with his other hand, but there was still tension on the line, and if he released the hook, it would sink in up to the shank. To make matters worse, he wore glasses to see the bank, but needed to take them off to look at objects up close. With both hands occupied, he couldn't see to unhook himself.

He didn't know that I had never before in my life been in a canoe. It's no wonder to me the Indians lost in those tipsy little things.

Later, I told Big C that he was really fortunate. The lure could have been a Lucky Thirteen.

So if some doctor isn't on time enough to suit you, and you need to blame someone, blame me. He was probably up all night working on me, Adam, or one of our comrades. And we were dog-gone glad he was there when we needed him.

Speaking of Adam, he's got what I call a "specialized" medical problem. Let me illustrate.

I had been sitting against the huge pecan for three hours, still as possible, camouflaged from boots to cap, a screen of leafy box elder branches stuck up around me. The paw-paws had leafed out, and the bull nettle was knee high, so visibility was a problem, but that's the way of turkey hunting on the Mississippi River. A gobbler had to be inside of forty yards before I could shoot at him anyway.

A turkey had gobbled at me a couple of times from the south nearly an hour before, and though my yelps and clucks were suitably sexy and turkily enticing, I had not heard or seen a thing since, except for a "Lawd God" bird (pileated woodpecker). Once more I cut my eyes to the right as far as I could, in case a turkey was sneaking in from the west. My left side was protected by a brush pile, since I shoot from the left shoulder.

A movement caught my eye; something dark. Turkey, deer, armadillo, raccoon, wolf? It disappeared behind a sycamore tree, and I swung my gun into position while whatever it was couldn't see me moving, just in case. I froze again.

Minutes later, the dark green bull nettle rippled by the sycamore, maybe thirty yards away. Whatever it was, I could only make out a dark back, quartering diagonally across the clearing. If it was a turkey, this was going to be a walk-by. But with the lay of the land on our river islands, it could just as easily be a deer feeding down a swag with its head down, or an armadillo doodling along a ridge.

This was a turkey. I saw the wings flex momentarily, but its head was still down. My heart was pounding, seemingly having jumped from my chest to between my ears. I had to breathe through my mouth as the bird moved toward a paw-paw thicket. Was it a hen feeding through, or a wary old gobbler who knew better than to raise his head in the open? It looked like I wasn't going to find out. In desperation, I summoned up a low "cluck."

One step from the paw-paw sanctuary, the turkey paused and raised its head six inches out of the bull nettle. The gun barrel was already aligned, the safety was off, my trigger finger was poised.

The head was fire-engine red!

I busted him. On the scale back at the cabin he weighed twenty-two pounds, and his beard, which I never saw until I picked him up, was eleven and a half inches long, one of the finest trophies in my gun cabinet. But if my son had been sitting under that old pecan that morning instead of me, he would have had to let that big gobbler walk off.

The boy is to some extent color-blind. Against the green paw-paw and bull nettle background, he could never have told that the turkey's head was red.

Color-blindness is an impairment that, by some estimates, appears in over twenty percent of the male population. I can think of no other vocation or avocation that would be more handicapped by this condition than that of Turkey Hunter.

Don't ask me why women aren't color-blind. I never answer questions about women. As a matter of fact, I have a great many questions about them myself. Send me answers if you have any.

At eighteen years of age, Adam finally found a solution, or at least a partial compensation for his condition, and he has given me permission to pass it on to the rest of the turkey hunting world. He found it quite by accident.

At an after-Christmas sale, he was looking at some shooting glasses and happened to try on a pair with vermillion-tinted lenses—rose-colored glasses, literally!

Reliable witnesses reported that the kid went plumb crazy. Suddenly, he was running around the store, pointing at this object and that one. "That's a red tie!" he exclaimed to a doctor who had dropped in for a new shotgun. "That's a green jacket!" the football coach was informed. "Your scarf is pink!" he yelled to a young lady buying ski boots, who ran into the stock room in case these new glasses also imparted x-ray vision. "Yellow!" "Blue!" "Orange!" "Purple!" were revealed to customers not wearing proper lenses. It was obviously a total revelation. For some, the world really does look better through Rose Colored Glasses.

Like Adam, I also have a "specialized" medical problem.

I shoot left-handed.

"No big deal," some of you may be saying. Well, it isn't if the southpaw has a double-barrel, over-under, or a bottom-ejection model. But I grew up during the days when a kid just learning to hunt got handed down his pappy's or grandpappy's old shotgun, and most of my male ancestors were right-handed. Big Robert tried to teach me to shoot thataway, but I couldn't hit the proverbial bull in the butt with the proverbial bass fiddle right-handed, and he finally gave up in exasperation just before I started cutting out paperdolls. Took him years to get over the embarrassment of having a kid who shot the wrong way.

However, as The Rule dictates, my sire used the excuse of breaking in a younger hunter to purchase himself a new shotgun, while the old gun was handed down to a kid who couldn't be trusted not to scratch the finish on the new double-barrel. The old pumpgun, one of my all-time favorites, was right-handed. At that point, no one knew any better. It was The Rule!

I grew up under the impression that, after shooting three boxes of shells on a dove hunt, *everybody* was deaf for the next two days!

You must understand that there was no malice aforethought on my elder's part. He just was not capable of seeing the problem because he did not have a southpaw's perspective. Since shooting did not deafen him, he just put my malady down to physical problems (and to some extent this was true), and adapted by speaking louder, especially during hunting season when the problem seemed to worsen. Fall is the time for weather-related allergies anyway, so this was understandable.

My parents tried home medical remedies: they'd rub me down with Vicks Salve at night, and make me eat carrots. It never improved my hearing, but at least when I slid greased-pig-like out of the top bunk, I could see to get back in the bed. I got eardrops and nosedrops, and had to gargle with Dr. Tichenors, which wasn't bad atall. They'd heat salt in a sock and I'd have to sleep with the sock on my ear. The standard remedy for croup was a teaspoon of sugar laced with coal-oil (now called kerosene), and I'll guarantee you that after one dose the patient dasn't croup again that night for love nor money!

As I matured, I outgrew the old Model 31 Remington, and hung it in a hallowed place on the den wall. I was ready to buy my own gun. At that time, seems like left-hand guns were not particularly in demand, and besides, they cost an arm and a leg. I purchased French Gun (a LaSalle pump) in a right-handed version, of course. Not only was I dodging the cost, but I really had no idea that the gun was a factor in my hearing loss. Remember, I thought everyone was a little deaf after a hunt.

My first inkling that my hunting might be different from others came when I had to visit an Ear, Nose, and Throat Specialist for another problem. My examination included a hearing test. When I came out of the phone booth outfit, the doctor, knowing I was a hunter, greeted me with, "I bet I can tell you which shoulder you shoot from!"

Only suckers take bets like that; "Left; but how'd you know?" I asked.

He showed me all kinds of little up-and-down lines on a graph and I knew that my bill was going to be on the up rather than the down line, all to the effect that my right ear was deaf as a post. "When you shoot a right-handed gun left-handed, you get a certain amount of blast effect in your right ear from the breech opening on that side. Your left ear is on the other side of the stock, so it isn't affected. You need to wear muffs or plugs if you're going to continue hunting," he concluded.

Great idea. But I was to learn that I never could find the durn things when I was going hunting, or else I'd forget them. Only time I'd remember to wear them was for chain-sawing. By this time, money was short, the baby needed shoes, and a left-handed gun was not in the budget. I grew used to cupping one hand behind my left ear and saying "Pardon me?" The back pew was no longer an option if there was any danger of the preacher calling on me for the closing prayer. I found that if I was close enough to hear a turkey gobble, I'd already scared him off the roost. My kids all learned the meaning of the word "Enunciate!"

Friends are wonderful things to have. One year Russ showed up for dove season with a brand-new left-handed pumpgun, and told me that I had no idea how much difference it made to his hearing. Truer words were never spoken. But money was still short, and besides, French Gun was like a member of the family.

Finally, Russ took matters into his own hands. A guy he knew had an almost-new left-handed Remington 870 that he wanted to get shut of. Russ bought it, telephoned Betsy, and informed her that he had just purchased my Christmas present, and did she want in on the deal? She did.

It was love at first blast. I retired French Gun, and christened the new pump "SouthPow." I think it's my last shotgun.

Really, the difference was like daylight and dark. Southpaw hunters, the other people in the dove field or duck blind do not have to be hollered at just because they hunt. There may be other reasons, but right-handed folks can usually hear fine during and after a hunt. Granted, changing guns may not cure a terminal case of the dumbs, but it can do wonders for the deafs!

Parents, listen to your Uncle Bob; whether your kid is fourteen or forty, if he is shooting a right-handed pumpgun or automatic from the left shoulder, go out tomorrow and get him a left-handed gun. Or at the very least, switch him to a double-barrel, an over-and-under, or a bottom-ejection gun.

That's not even a suggestion. That's an order!

Well, all the foregoing was kid stuff, I realized a couple of years ago. I mean, when you finally figure out you obviously have an incurable affliction that's going to be fatal, it sure brings you down to earth and puts things in perspective.

Mine had to be bone cancer. I consulted my grandfather's old *Merck's Manual*, and our new *Readers' Digest Family Health Encyclopedia*, and that's the only answer I could come up with that was anywhere close to suiting my symptoms.

For several months, I had been noticing that my arms had been slowly growing shorter; shrinking in length, as it were. It seemed to be especially bad in the evenings on days when I had been either writing or reading a lot. By the time I got the writing pad far enough away to be able to see the words, I couldn't reach it with the pencil. And the best way to read the evening paper was to throw the paper on the floor, then sit down in my chair and read it.

I endured this condition heroically for a long time, for the only real pain involved was when I sunk a couple of fishhooks in my hand trying to get the Jitterbug far enough away to stick the monofilament through the eye of the lure. Switching to colored line seemed to help a lot, by the way. Someone in the tackle industry should have figured out that fishing line that is invisible to the fish is also invisible to fishermen whose arms are too short as a result of bone cancer.

Though I don't make a habit of it, I occasionally have to make emergency repairs if a button comes loose. When you have my type of bone cancer, threading a needle is well-nigh impossible. Those little gold safety pins work much better, I found. I did gain an understanding of the parable of putting a camel through the eye of a needle, though: at least one can see the dang camel. And I stood just as good a chance of threading a camel as the thread itself.

Finally, I screwed up my courage and went to see Doctor Carl. I mean, there are certain arrangements to be made in these cases: color of roses, whether I was going to make it one more turkey season, etc. Trying to break it to my friend as gently as possible, I explained my symptoms and my diagnosis.

Well, he got this smug, wise expression on his face, scrawled something illegibly on a little pink paper, and sent me next door.

It was a miracle! Doctor Bill next door fitted those things on my head, and immediately my arms returned to their former length! I snatched up a magazine and flipped through it, elbows bent. I wrote something legibly on a notepad, elbow bent. I wrote him a check for the eyeglasses, elbow bent.

No bone cancer; just normal aging, the learned men said.

Those of us who have birthdays around New Years sometimes get a double dose of thoughts concerning the passage of time. I have thunk a few of these thoughts myself, some of them last rabbit season. In case you may not be familiar with some of the problems the older generation of hunters face, let me try to explain.

For instance, in a family where several members hunt, a gun cabinet might hold the following gauge shotguns: .410, .28, .20, .16, .12, and even .10. All these shotguns use different size shells, I'm sure you know.

Some shotshell manufacturers color-code their shells: red for twelves, purple for sixteen, yellow for twenty—and these entrepreneurs will undoubtedly go to heaven on the first train. The others, however, stamp the number on the brass end of the shell. (Of course, one doesn't need to look at *all* the shells. Even a golfer can tell a .410 from a ten gauge!)

Every well-laid-out gun cabinet has a drawer where hunters dump their left-over shells at the end of the hunt. While sorting through this drawer, I began noticing that most ammo makers were obviously stamping the gauge numbers in smaller print than in years previous. Evidently this was a marketing strategy to try to force hunters to buy new shells when they couldn't tell what size the old ones jumbled up in the drawer were.

In many cases, this strategy is successful. The first time a hunter goes rabbit hunting with sixteen gauge shells and a twelve gauge gun, especially if his partner is shooting a twenty gauge, he will gladly pay four prices for a brand-new box that says "twelve gauge" in big letters on three sides.

The younger generation, not being set in their ways, has apparently learned to read those stamped-in-brass symbols by feel, or the Braille system. B.C. and Adam seem to be able to sort shells quite easily, but my old calloused fingers can't quite learn the knack. However, once I *have* been able to sort my gauges correctly, the battle isn't even half over.

For every hunter uses several different shot sizes in, for instance, a twelve gauge shotgun. Maybe nines for quail, eights for doves, sixes for squirrels, fives for rabbits, fours for ducks, and twos for turkeys. Used to be, the manufacturers would print the shot size in large numbers on two sides of each shell. But now, I find that shot size (indeed, all printing on the shells) is apparently being printed in Navajo. Blurred Navajo. Small, blurred Navajo.

I am sure the Navajo tribe will be eternally grateful, but what about those of us who read only English and a little dimly-remembered high-school Latin?

I don't mean to give anyone the impression that physical infirmities brought about by the aging process have anything at all to do with these problems. As I have pointed out, these are just examples of successful marketing ploys by conniving corporate conglomerates. My point is simply that a generation of hunters can remember when ammo manufacturers used to print bigger, and in English. Things are different nowadays.

After we hit the fields to hunt, I am reminded once more of something else that's different. Medical science, for all the wonderful repairs it has bestowed on my body over the years, still has challenges to be met for those of us who insist on hunting after healing. The sooner these problems are understood and corrected, the better it will be for all mankind.

Now you just take nerves, for example. When a surgeon does a knee reconstruction job, there is apparently one little nerve he overlooks during repairs. This is the nerve that signals height to the brain. When one is crossing field and forest in pursuit of game, it is necessary for the brain to be in constant communication with the feet. Ditches have to be jumped; logs must be stepped over; vines must be negotiated. I couldn't help noticing that there was now a two-inch error factor in my own bodily head-to-foot conversation. The brain would say, "Lift up six inches for that obstacle," yet the foot was always two inches short of clearance.

Ditches that seemed to call for a three-foot jump only got a two-foot ten-incher. It had to be that knee operation a few years ago.

Rudely, my companions commented that my gun barrel was often that same two inches off when it came to connecting with the rabbits as well. I pointed out that their youth, ignorance, and inexperience made them insensitive to the problems of seasoned sportsmen, and that either the broken wrist or the shoulder separation could have caused similar nerve misconnections.

Old injuries also interrupt in some manner the ability of the bodily thermostats to adjust. I am convinced that on cold days, I am at least four inches shorter than on warm days. And when cold and warm happen the same day, it feels like my body is an accordion on which someone is playing "The Wreck Of Old 97."

We've established that hunting often is responsible for the injuries that affect our aim in later years. When I was my companions' age, I associated dance season with hunting season. Seems that there was a dance within an hour's drive nearly every night during the springtime, and "jukin'" then had a much more obligatory connotation to me than it does now.

But this was also during one of those winters when the ducks were down in droves, and here too was an obligation that could not be ignored. Fortunately, dance times and duck times don't conflict—unless one needs to sleep, that is. For a week my schedule was thus: bathe and dress by six; pick up date by seven; date is ready at eight; supper before dance begins at nine; dance until one; attend breakfast until two; home by three; change from tux to camouflage, brew coffee, and leave for the river by four; hunt from sunup until noon; home, lunch, clean ducks, and catch a nap before arising to bathe for that night's dance.

I always thought the exhaust fumes got to me, but somehow the jeep ended up in the ditch while returning from the river one day. I was looking at that particular scar while shaving recently, and the dozen stitches now blend in nicely with my other wrinkles.

There had been a dance last night before this rabbit hunt, too, and I couldn't help but think of how the times have changed. Instead of getting up at the crack of dawn, we had rolled out about the crack of ten. That, we can probably blame on Daylight Savings Time. Of course, in many areas there are hardly enough ducks left to hunt; the rabbits are in the fields at all hours, and beagles will run whenever you open the pen. Still, it really seems to me that either the nights used to be longer, or at least one could do a lot more sleeping in a lot less time.

Back in those days, mud was not as sticky, either. Slopes were not as steep, ditches not as wide, air was not as hard to breathe, and quail flew a lot slower when flushed. The beagles had run through a covey just ahead, and the birds were out of range before I got my gun up. Guns and shells in the old days used to be lighter to carry, but conversely, seems like the shells had more shot in them back then. On the other hand, today's rabbits are a great deal heavier than those we used to kill and carry home when I was younger.

We had been in the field about an hour when the rain began, and that's different now, too. I swear I can remember when rain used to be soft and faintly warmish, rather like cooking oil. One could hunt all day in a comfortable drizzle. But this rain, though not a hard shower, was a harsh, raw, chilling rain. Aggressive, too; it went right to work and trickled down the back of my neck, quickly finding its way below the belt and to the vicinity of the long john flap. Not only did the rain attack from the rear, but it also made a frontal assault, running down my shirt collar and matting the chest hairs into a cold, gray paste. That was a change, too; the color of chest hair, I mean. Must be that Acid Rain we read about.

We called up the dogs—the fire had already been taken care of—and I beat everybody home to a warm shower and a hot cup of coffee with a dollop of anti-gray-chest-hair medicine in it. This is not a usual practice, but the occasion seemed to call for it.

Used to be, preparations for a hunt included only weapons, ammo, knives, boots, and appropriate clothes; nowadays there are different considerations:

1) Two Re-Heater packs: the small one for the bad hand, and the large one for back and neck;

2) Choose between the metal knee brace and the elastic one;

3) Find the whirlpool before leaving, so as not to have to climb the stairs for it after the hunt.

4) Check the medical belt pouch for the proper quantities of aspirin, eye drops, Alka-Seltzer, Lomotil, Band-Aids, iodine, etc. Whole platoons have gone into combat with less medical supplies.

There is one analgesic ointment called Icy Hot that smells so loud that deer are able to detect it from a half-mile upwind; yet at times, this is an acceptable risk. Other products may be less odoriferous, but I have always been convinced that healing properties are in direct proportion to smell and sting. As the saying goes, "No pain, no gain." We may be getting older, but the alternative is still just as unattractive.

Dance bands ain't the same either. I had the night before seldom heard a slow dance piece, a trend I have noticed for several years. Personally, if I am dancing with a lovely lady, I see little sense in dancing six feet away from her! And the volume at which modern bands feel obligated to play leaves me in the same state as after a four-hour artillery barrage. Had this been turkey season, I couldn't have heard a gobbler this morning if I had been roosting in the same tree!

But the girls were as pretty as ever, I had observed. Thank the Lord that some things never change. As a salute to that thought, I poured another dram of anti-gray-chest-hair medicine and pulled my rocker closer to the fire.

Postscript to this chapter:

Just in case you may be saying, "Surely he'll grow out of it," let me assure you that the condition seems permanent.

I was over in the office printing out the last two chapters of this book, when I heard a soft "Whhooommpp!" and looked across the patio to see our kitchen in flames, all the way up to the twelve-foot ceilings. A skillet of grease had vaporized and exploded.

Betsy and I managed to get the blaze out with the fire hose (something no country home should be without) after I had thrown the pot of grease outside, in the process acquiring serious burns to my right hand and arm. Betsy was unhurt, and the kitchen was nearly totaled, but we saved the house.

After the excitement was over, she called Doctor Tom, who simply said, "I'll meet him down at the office." By nine o'clock he had me on my way again, complete with antibiotics, pain pills, a tetnus shot, and swathed in bandages. The burns on my hand approached third degree, and would require careful attention in order to heal, then some rehabilitation, he informed me as he relocked the office door.

No sweat, I figured as I got in the van. Very few patients have as much experience in the art of healing as I do.

Practice, practice, practice!

Russ

FAST EDDIE, MATILDA, AND THE LAST WEEKEND WALTZ

"Now, it's gonna be tough this last weekend of the season," Johnny Mac warned me long distance. "The gobblers that are left by now are the ones that have beaten us all season long: the Devil Birds!"

I grinned. "I'll take my chances. It'll be good to hunt with you again. I appreciate the invitation. But now, listen!" I insisted. "I know you've been guiding all season, but this is the last weekend. If I'm coming, we're both hunting!"

Johnny Mac and I had hunted together for years on Woodstock Island in the Mississippi River. Then he had been transferred to South Mississippi by his insurance company, and we had been unable to get together for turkey season in more than ten years. Now, however, my old friend worked as a guide for Robin Callendar's Cedar Ridge Guided Hunts in Port Gibson. Cedar Ridge was more than a two-hour drive south for me, but less than an hour west of Jackson, where my son was a freshman at Millsaps College. Adam was on the baseball team and he and I had been unable to hunt together this spring, but baseball had ended now; this was our last chance.

"Let Adam come on in from Jackson, and you just meet him here," the guide urged. "Leave everything else to Robin and me. But be ready," he cautioned again, "those Devil Birds are gonna turn you every which way but loose!"

Adam and I arrived at the Cedar Ridge lodge just before dark on Friday evening. A familiar group of men was already assembled, waiting for Jack Partridge to serve his famous venison spaghetti. In addition to Robin and Johnny Mac, there was Jack Wood, local landowner and president of the Mississippi Wild Turkey Federation; Zac Whaley, a director of the Mississippi Bowhunters' Association; guides Tommy Sutton and Keith Partridge; Dr. Curtis Bonin of New Orleans; and two Texans who were at Cedar Ridge to hunt Russian boar. Zac often helped as a guide, and also had an eighteen-year-old son; he immediately volunteered to put Adam on a gobbler. "We'll go after Fast Eddie," he declared. "This kid might be just the one to put the whammy on that old Devil Bird!"

Four-thirty a.m. came too quickly, but Jack had coffee, eggs, bacon, and biscuits steaming for his hunters. He had hardly been to bed, it seemed. I reiterated to Johnny Mac and Zac that Adam and I, though unfamiliar with the territory, were friendship hunters and expected them to take advantage of any last-weekend opportunities.

Johnny Mac shoved his empty plate back and motioned for me to finish my third cup of coffee. "Time to go, fella. We got a date with the Devil Bird of Sam Hill!"

Tommy Sutton grinned as he poured another cup; he and Dr. Bonin didn't have as far to go. "You know that a gobbler's got your number when you've hunted him long enough to name him!" he jibed.

And did he have our number! He gobbled immediately to Johnny's hooting, sounding like he was half a mile away. We took off down the logging road in the darkness, pausing now and then to evoke another gobble. "I know right where he's roosted," my companion declared. But as we hustled down the dim road, suddenly the old bird shook the woods less than a hundred yards away!

"I don't know how in the heck he got there," Johnny Mac whispered in exasperation. "I just hope he hasn't heard us walking. Let's ease back fifty yards and set up."

The gobbler sounded off on his own another dozen times in the tree, then answered from his limb to Johnny Mac's soft tree yelp. After the turkey hit the ground, though, there was dead silence in response to our calls. We were almost ready to move when there was a heart-stopping gobble just over the edge of the hill—barely fifty yards away. It sounded like the Devil Bird of Sam Hill was fixing to step into the road right in front of a load of twelve gauge sixes.

We froze in breathless anticipation, hearts in our throats. The minutes dragged by. Finally, my guide tried a soft cluck. Then another, louder.

He gobbled again, two hundred yards away and getting further!

"Dadgum it! He's headed off the end of the ridge and toward the creek bottom! C'mon! If we hustle, we can head him off!"

Each carrying twenty extra—both pounds and years—we alternately trotted and walked down our ridge and around another. Every time we paused for breath, Johnny would blow his crow call, and the Devil Bird would gobble back from afar.

Our pace slowed. "We're way ahead of him," my guide said as we approached the end of the ridge. "We'll set up and..." There was a thunderous gobble less than seventy-five yards dead ahead of us, just over the ridge.

We dropped flat in the logging road, but we probably should have charged. "How in the..." my friend agonized, but interrupted himself to plan tactics. "Crawl over behind that tree while I sneak back down the road calling. This time, if he stops before he gets within range of the calling position, you can fix his clock!"

Minutes later, I heard him yelp from a hundred yards away. No reply. After a short pause, he gave another series of yelps. Total silence from in front of me. But suddenly a shot boomed from behind!

I heard the sound of a turkey flopping, and rose to congratulate my buddy. But it was not the long-bearded Devil Bird of Sam Hill that Johnny Mac hoisted for my attention. It was a jake.

"Three of 'em came running up from the other direction," he explained sheepishly, "and I figured a jake in the hand is worth a Devil Bird walking off down the creek bottom laughing at us. Guess I was tired of getting outsmarted. I still don't see how that old scoundrel got in front of us so quick!"

Back at the lodge, we found another small first-year gobbler hanging in the walk-in cooler, alongside the hog hunters' trophy. Another sheepishly grinning guide 'fessed up. "I couldn't help it," Zac contended. "It was reflex. I *had* to shoot him!"

Robin calmly contradicted him. "Naw. You could have let him go." Turned out that a big gobbler had shortstopped Zac and Adam before they got into Fast Eddie's territory by responding to Zac's hoots. After toying with the hunters for a while from his limb, this Devil Bird had sailed down just out of gun range and gobbled his head off.

While the Tom was ringing the woods from the tree, Zac said he had asked Adam, "Are you excited?"

"No, sir," was the calm answer.

"But when that gobbler sounded off from the ground right in front of us, your boy leaned over and whispered, 'N-n-n-n-*now* I'm excited!'" Zac chuckled to me.

However, their Devil Bird had done just like ours had; when the hen refused to come the short distance to him, the gobbler had turned and walked off down the ridge, rattling back at the pleading calls every few minutes until he was almost out of hearing. The guide had decided to circle, motioning Adam to follow him away from the gobbler.

But the hunters had only taken a few steps when a half-dozen heads popped up over the ridge. One of them was red, and Zac, in the lead, had reacted accurately. Turkeys had exploded into the air, except for the flopping jake, and the young hunter had swung his gun up.

The guide had previously been warned that Adam was color blind and couldn't tell a gobbler's head from a hen's unless he had plenty of time. Zac ducked and began to yell, watching the gun barrel: "Don't shoot! That's a hen!... I'm sorry!... Hen again!... I'm sorry!... Not that one!... I didn't mean to!... Wait! Another hen!... I'm sorry I shot!"

None of the other turkeys had been a gobbler, and it was probably a good thing. Adam was rolling on the ground laughing at his guide's abject apologies before the rest of the flock was out of sight. "I couldn't have gotten a shot off anyway," he reported.

"Jakes are a guide's best friend!" Robin drawled laconically. "Tell 'em about the Polish immigrant you guided last year, Zac."

A natural storyteller, Whaley gladly obliged. "Took the guy out before daylight, hooted, and a jake gobbled a hundred yards away. We blinded in, waited until daylight, and I yelped one series. That li'l ole bird flew down almost in our laps, and I punched the guy and said 'Shoot!' We were back at the lodge drinking coffee by 6:30.

"That fella looked at that gobbler, looked at me, and said, 'Ees nossing to dees thurrkey honting, vot?'" The group roared with laughter.

After Zac had killed the jake, he and Adam had gone after Fast Eddie. The boy said he knew this Devil Bird was different when the guide paused before climbing the ridge to sprinkle them both with water from a pint Wild Turkey decanter. "This is my lucky charm," he had confided. "It'll protect us. Don't you feel warmer?" Adam nodded. Of course, it was about ten o'clock. "No, that's not why it's hotter here; this is Fast Eddie's territory." The guide sniffed the air. "Smell that brimstone?"

They had ventured less than a quarter-mile into Fast Eddie's territory when Zac yelled, jumped straight up, and came down stomping madly. Trembling, he finally backed up and pointed a

shaking finger at a small rattlesnake in its death throes. "See?" he had said shakily, "To get to Fast Eddie, you have to walk through rattlesnakes!"

The boy told me later that as they advanced down the ridge, the guide would stop now and then to point out a spot. "See that stump (or tree, or clearing)? That's one of the places where he did it to me!"

In a small clearing, there were fresh coyote droppings in the logging road. As they paused to examine the spoor, Adam had asked Zac, "Why do you call him Fast Eddie?"

"Just around that bend, I was set up with a client one time, and Eddie had gobbled at us from out front. Then he took rounders and without warning, suddenly came zipping by our tree from behind, almost close enough to touch. When the client moved to get his gun up, the turkey just circled the tree at full speed and left in the same direction he came from. Durn client almost shot me trying to swing on him. We've called him Fast Eddie ever since."

A hundred yards down the road, the guide had blinded in. "How do you know this is a good place?" the youngster whispered.

"You hear that?" Whaley responded in a hushed tone.

"No, sir," the boy breathed.

"There you go," Zac murmured. "You know it's Fast Eddie when you don't hear him gobble!"

And sure enough, they related to us at the lodge, Fast Eddie had done it to them again. After an hour of fruitless calling, they had arisen to return for lunch. And right next to the pile of coyote dung they had paused at earlier, was a smoking pile of fresh gobbler droppings.

Robin laughed. "Fast Eddie's got Zac's number so bad that he doesn't deposit his droppings in a 'J' any more. Now he leaves them in a 'Z' shape!"

"Even worse," Zac agreed, "was the time he took his time and spelled my name out. He even put a 'K' on it to make me mad!"

"Those Devil Birds get the guides so frustrated by the season's end that I've thought seriously about a napalm bombing raid. Most all of our clients get a shot at a turkey, but those old gobblers can take care of themselves," Robin declared as Jack Partridge called us to lunch.

I was in for a new experience that afternoon. I had never hunted turkeys with a decoy before. As we left the truck to cross one of Jack Wood's pastures, Johnny Mac reached in the back for a sack. "Lemme introduce you to Matilda," he said.

As we walked, he explained that sometimes decoys evoke totally different reactions from turkeys. "I've seen big gobblers actually try to mount the things; yet at other times, I've seen jakes walk into the edge of a field, take one look at the decoy, and head back for the woods at a dead run. But on the last weekend, you try everything you know about."

We arrived at an old blind next to a fence corner. "Made some good videos here," my friend opined. I began to clear the dead cane away as he shoved Matilda's stake into the ground. Standing, he looked at his watch. "Quarter to five. We've got time to take a nap. The turkeys come into this field at six."

We made ourselves comfortable behind the fence, and I loaded my Remington SouthPow as he got out a couple of calls. I had barely finished applying camo grease and Johnny Mac had just put on his head net and reached for the mosquito spray when he glanced into the field.

"There's your gobbler, Bob," he said calmly.

It had to be a trick, but his accomplice would have had a better chance of fooling me if he had waited until the guide had at least called once. A realistic-looking gobbler was half-strutting ten steps from Matilda. Must be some kind of balloon decoy-on-a-pulley arrangement, I figured detachedly.

"Shoot!" hissed my guide. But I wasn't falling for a stunt like this. I didn't even raise my gun. "Shoot!" he urged in an undertone. I started to grin. Can't fool old Neill.

Then the gobbler went into full strut!

I busted him. He never saw me raise the gun. His full attention was riveted on Matilda. In all my years, I have never so nonchalantly bagged a turkey. I didn't have time to even think about missing him!

"Seven minutes!" Johnny Mac exclaimed, dancing around the trophy bird. The beard was over ten inches long and the spurs were more than an inch and had begun to curve upward. "Seven minutes!" my friend shouted again, and hugged me.

Stepping back, he echoed Zac Whaley's punch line with a huge smile. "Ees nossing to dees thurrkey honting, vot?"

THE TATTERED FAN

The opening weekend of deer season was almost here, and as usual I was packed early. And as usual, S.P. was late. With the kids in school and Betsy at work, I paced nervously that Friday afternoon, re-checking my duffel bag, grocery box, and ice chest. I cleaned and sorted through a year's accumulation of shotgun shells and rifle cartridges in the box under the gun cabinet, noticing that I had to put on my reading glasses to tell 30.06 from 30.30, or sixteen from twenty gauge. I hadn't needed to do that last year; time marches on.

The outdoor books on the shelves by the guns had gotten jumbled, so I rearranged them, flipping through to an occasional favorite passage. Yet I glanced impatiently at my watch more than the books. My old college roomie had said he'd come rolling in between two and three, and from past experience I knew it would be much closer to the latter than the former. Still an hour to go.

I got the stepladder and changed a couple of light bulbs that Betsy had been after me to replace for two months. As long as I had the ladder out anyway, I decided to go ahead and retire the old turkey fan on the den wall. It had been up there a

long time and had begun to look disreputable—
tattered and moth-eaten. Since Zac had made me a
new one from the big gobbler I had killed last
spring, maybe this old fan should be just thrown
away, as Betsy had suggested.

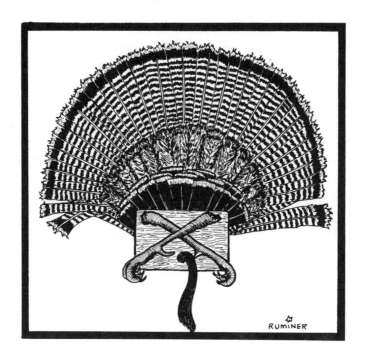

RUMINER

The display of spread tailfeathers, crossed legs,
and jutting heavy beard had been a trophy from
my first gobbler; and as I lifted it from the wall,
memories flooded back. I had just turned fifteen
when I had made this display myself. The sharp-
pointed spurs on the crossed legs were over an
inch long, and the thick beard measured an even

twelve inches. In thirty years of turkey hunting, I had only brought home two gobblers that were as good as this one, and somehow I hated to take the ragged thing off the wall.

Big Robert and Mr. Hurry had dropped me off at the dim old logging road a full two hours before daylight, warning me to be sure I had my raingear. The muted rumble of thunder in the west foretold the approaching front, but this was no deterrent to turkey hunters. "Every gobbler in the woods oughta sound off when this thunder gets closer. Good luck!" Mr. Hurry said as he put the jeep in gear. The headlight beam disappeared around a bend headed for the old log dump on the other side of the island.

I used my flashlight as little as possible as I made my way into the woods, following the dim logging road for almost a half-mile until I came to the huge old pecan tree I planned to be blinded in under at daylight. Arranging a few paw-paw branches in front of me, I sprayed me, branches, and tree with "skeeter scoot" and settled back to await the dawn.

It was a long wait, but the chorus of nearby owls, accompanied by the bass rumblings and the glowing flashes of the oncoming weather front kept me from being bored. It was going to be a race to see if daylight would beat the storm. Then my nose told me that I had a visitor. In the bluish momentary illumination from a faraway bolt of lightning, I saw a skunk ambling my way.

The critter was close and I froze, knowing that if I didn't disturb him, there would be no problem. Or so I thought. The undisturbed little black-and-white feline began puttering around in a downed treetop less than fifteen feet from me! I gritted my teeth and sat motionless, aware that the faint stench I now smelled would be multiplied a thousandfold if I moved and alarmed the skunk, who had apparently found a week's worth of groceries right in front of me.

I had become so absorbed in skunk-watching that I had failed to notice the storm's progress, and I nearly jumped at a sudden clap of thunder. I was barely able to control a second movement when a booming gobble sounded—in the tree right over me!

There has never been a longer half-hour before daylight. Thunder boomed, lightning bolts crashed around us, the turkey gobbled at every sound louder than my pounding heart, and the skunk scratched about in the decaying limbs as if it were at a Sunday School picnic. Day dawned before the storm broke, finally showing me The Boss Gobbler of Montgomery Island actually strutting up and down one of the larger limbs of the pecan tree, gobbling his head off.

It was a terrible thing to do; horrible, unforgivable. I should have been tried, convicted, tarred, feathered, and run out of town on a rail. Yet I submit to the reader that a plea of insanity is clearly, even obviously, justified: my tender age, the threatening storm, the stinky nearby skunk, and the loudest, biggest gobbler in the woods less than twenty-five yards from a young hunter who had never shot a wild turkey.

Thunderclap and shotgun blast blended, but it was the concussion from the latter that galvanized the skunk into action. Yet my youth and excitement made it a close match. When I fired, I not only jumped to my feet, but I jumped clean over the skunk. A ghastly odor flooded the woods behind me as I sprinted to the flopping turkey.

It was my first gobbler. The storm broke almost immediately, and there was no way I was going to let that magnificent bird get wet. Wrapping the turkey in my rainsuit, I walked the two miles to camp in the downpour cradling my trophy, which never got a drop on one feather. For thirty years after, that big gobbler's fan, spurs, and beard had graced my wall.

And probably would have continued to, had S.P. been on time today. As I descended the ladder with the fan in my hand, I noticed that the cypress wall in the den had faded just enough that I could still see the outline of the fan where it had hung for so many years. "Hope the one Zac fixed for me is big enough to cover that spot," I muttered.

"I hear when you get old you start talking to yourself," a voice boomed, startling me out of my reverie. S.P. stood in the doorway, grinning. "I thought we were going deer hunting. What are you doing with that turkey tail?"

"Aw, it's gettin' old and moth-eaten, falling apart like a couple of old football players I know that oughta be taking a nurse with them to deer camp," I replied. I held up the trophy. "Looks kinda ragged, doesn't it? It's so old, some of the feathers just broke half in two, looks like."

A strange look came over my friend's face. "Those feathers didn't break off because of age," he declared. "Nobody's told you what happened to them?" Then he answered his own question, "Obviously not."

"What are you talking about?" I was mystified.

S.P. perched on the arm of the sofa. "That spring when your daddy died and we were all here for the funeral, the undertaker got all of us pallbearers together in this room to instruct us before the services. And then he pinned some little ole white flowers on our suit lapels."

When he paused I injected, "I wasn't noticing much about them, but that's what pallbearers usually wear, isn't it?"

S.P. nodded. "Reckon so. But they're not particularly pretty, and don't have any smell atall, like Russ said that day. Somehow those little white flowers seemed too impersonal. Just not appropriate whatsoever for somebody that loved the outdoors like Big Robert did."

He pointed at the barstool I kept by the bookcase. "Right after Russ said that, Dude told me to hold that stool for him where you've got that ladder right now. Suit and all, he climbed up there, got out his pocketknife, and cut each of us a two-inch piece of wild turkey tailfeather out of that fan you're holding. Ten of us, ten feathers. We pinned them on as a backing behind those little white flowers on our lapels. Somehow that felt right for your daddy."

After a short silence, S.P. sighed and stood. "Well, are you ready to go deer hunting? We've got to cross the Mississippi River before dark."

I nodded. "I'm packed. Be ready as soon as I hang this old beat-up fan back on the wall. You mind holding this ladder for a second?"

"YOU WANT ME TO STICK MY HAND WHERE?!!"

Several years ago, a group of us "young" (still able to get out of bed in the mornings without medical attention) adults held a church fellowship skiing party on one of the big oxbow lakes. During the course of the festivities, the party raft where most of us roosted while the ski boats were operating out on the lake drifted close to the flooded willows. Our pastor, a young adult himself, spied a gallon jug floating about thirty yards away and volunteered to swim out and bring it back "before one of the ski boats comes back and hits it."

Well, Mike did that. He swam right out to that jug and grabbed it with both hands, when suddenly the jug decided to depart all by itself. The preacher began a determined side-kick back to the barge, but the look of determination quickly changed to a look of consternation as he realized he was getting further away from us! Tiring and panicked, he clutched the floating jug even tighter, but the jug just picked up speed. By the time the preacher realized that he had latched onto some jug-fisherman's catfish, he was nearly too far away to swim back to the raft.

Except for the fact that his congregation stood in unison at this point and shouted...not "Hallelujah!" but "JAWS! Dum Dum Dum Dum Dum....!" Mike nearly walked on the water.

We never found out how large our minister's catfish was. I later asked a local catfishing expert how big it might have been.

"The biggest I ever caught weighed about forty pounds," he opined, "but my daddy once caught one that weighed nearly ninety! 'Course, your preacher might have latched onto a seventy-five-pound snapping turtle. Sometimes you'll catch a small catfish on a jug and a big turtle will eat the fish and get hooked himself. If so, God must have been looking out for your church, 'cause a sho'nuff big loggerhead could have taken his leg off!"

That was pure-D speaking the truth. When I was just a little boy I was sitting on the bank of the Brownspur canal watching three men catfishing by another method: grabbling. To grabble, a wading fisherman must run his hand up into hollow logs or holes in the bank and pull out whatever he feels in there. (In my own humble opinion, grabblers must be either very brave, very crazy, very drunk—or all of the above!) One of these men reached into a hole in the bank, screamed, and jerked! Out of the hole, with a death grip on the guy's middle finger, flew a plate-sized snapping turtle as the man spun in agony with his arm extended full length. At the end of the swing, the loggerhead came loose and sailed almost to my bank before splashing into the canal—with two joints of the fisherman's middle finger still locked in his jaws!

I've never been tempted to grabble.

Probably the main methods of catfishing are jugfishing, trotlines, set hooks, and rod and reel. Well, except for seining. As most Mississippians are aware, there are currently over 100,000 acres of commercial catfish ponds in the state, so poundage-wise, seines undoubtedly catch more catfish than any other form of tackle. If you fish by this method, though, be sure you own the pond. Rustling catfish in this area is frowned upon by the law just as much as rustling cattle was in the old West.

Sometimes an enterprising catfish farmer will designate a certain pond as a "fish-for-pay" pond, and this provides an excellent opportunity for fast sport, good eating, and breaking in a young fisherman. Take along a small sack of dry dog food, cast a handful upon the waters, and smear a top-water bass plug with some of the foulest-smelling bait concoctions available. Then cast the plug into the middle of the floating dog food nuggets. In no time at all, catfish weighing three to five pounds will rise to the feed and will hit just like bass; some folks think they'll out-fight a largemouth.

One year our family hosted a Norwegian exchange student and, among other things, introduced him to Mississippi hunting and fishing. Adam took Johan over to Frank's catfish pond one afternoon, and I followed a half-hour later with a couple of iceboxes. We were to find that at least one Scandinavian had a unique concept of landing fish.

Johan quickly caught on to casting, but reeling was somehow difficult for our Viking to grasp. He solved the problem in style, though. He'd cast out, get a bite, set the hook with the Viking equivalent of the McElwee Hoist, then turn, hold the rod over his shoulder, and run like a striped ape down the side of the dike and across the pasture. The poor fish must have felt like the guy with his suspenders caught on the side window of the Corvette when the light changed! But it worked.

While catfishing with rod and reel may get fast and furious, the other methods are generally more laidback. When he was less than ten years old, Adam spent his spring afternoons after school running a line of set hooks close to a couple of beaver dams on the same canal where the grabbler lost his finger. The little catfish he brought in weren't more than three-quarters of a pound, but they were just right for a fillet knife, and the young man proudly fed the family on his catch several times until a big rain washed out the dams and set hooks one night.

In my own experience, catfishing has usually been a nighttime fun excursion. Two boats of us would ease along a slack water cut or "chute" of the Mississippi, baiting and dropping jugs. Then we'd motor downstream to a sandbar where the cut narrowed, collect driftwood, and build a roaring bonfire. Out would come the icebox with the food, everything from hot dogs and hamburgers to venison and duck. Now and then a jug would come bobbing by and a couple of us would run for the boat and chase it down. By midnight, a catfish of around five pounds would get skinned and slapped on a grill over a bed of slow coals. With a good baste of lemon, butter, and Worchestershire and frequent turning, this size fish cooks in about an hour, and cannot be beat for taste by the finest restaurants anywhere. It's ready to eat right before it falls through the grill!

You can get all kinds of disagreements about which species of catfish tastes the best. I've heard men swear by blue cats, yellow cats, channel cats, spoonbill cats, even the grunting saltwater "trash" fish of the Gulf Coast, the gafftop catfish. For my money, the best kind is the one in the pan, on the grill, or in the oven at the time the subject comes up, especially if Dude is doing the cooking!

Speaking of gafftops, let me relate a strange bit of first aid that they say works on all catfish, but it was a gafftop that got it demonstrated on me.

Adam and I were fishing the Gulf oil rigs below the mouth of the river with Ted Daly, "Admiral" Gene Drake, and Dude when the Admiral hooked a gafftop and swung it into the boat, where it landed fin-down on the top of my foot. The fin went through the tennis shoe and half an inch into my instep. We're talking excruciating pain here. Tears. Naughty words. All the worse because this is certain infection and rotting flesh. Everyone knows that.

Ted took charge. "Adam, get some ice in that towel. Gene, hold onto that fish; gotta use the one that stuck him. Dude, get your knife out. Bob, get your shoe off."

The Admiral stretched the gafftop out while Dude, at Ted's direction, carefully scraped a goodly blob of slime from the belly of the fish: "Got to be the same one that stabbed him," the expert emphasized again. My foot was already on fire and I wasn't at all enthusiastic about the impending treatment.

Dude tenatively spread the stuff around the throbbing, swelling wound. "Not good enough," Ted admonished, "Smear it around and down in the hole." Dude glanced at me nervously, but by now I was beyond caring. He mopped the slime on and worked it in with his knife blade.

"Now, Adam, lay that bag of ice on your daddy's foot and keep it on there," came the order. I was in serious pain; if he had come up with an axe, it would have spelled relief about then! Adam slapped the ice on and held the foot still. I felt like I had fever already. I didn't look, for I knew my foot must have begun to turn green. Ted calmly went back to casting.

In twenty minutes, it was healed.

I ain't claiming it'll work on anyone else. I ain't sure it worked on me. Could have been the beer Dude spilled on the ice. Could have been the salt air. Could have been voodoo. Could have been prayer. But whatever it was worked and I was back fishing again in half an hour.

So catfish fins are definitely worth avoiding. One of the quickest learners in this category, with probably the most unusual catfishing method of all, was a yellow male Labrador retriever named Mike, owned by my Godfather and neighbor, Frank Tindall. Mike was riding in the truck one day when Frank stopped and picked up a couple of handfuls of spilled catfish food and pitched it in the pond. The retriever reacted instinctively, and reached the food from the top just as a five-pound fish reached it from below. Mike dutifully grabbed the catfish and delivered it to his surprised owner, enduring a couple of painful finnings along the way.

"But he loved it," declared Frank, "and learned to grab the fish right behind the fin so it couldn't swing around and jab him. Mike never brings back a fish less than five pounds now," he brags. The Lab has even been on TV.

Trotlining is another popular method of catfishing, but not for me, at least not any longer. I had a bad experience with a trotline one night, and will wear the scars to my grave.

Nowadays, nylon trotlines are outlawed or restricted in many states. But not soon enough for me. Several years ago, more than a dozen couples from our church choir had gone to a river sandbar for a bonfire, camp supper, guitar pickin', and singalong. After we had built the bonfire, Ed Loudon, Chief McMaster, and I headed to the nearby willow brake to cut sticks for hot dog and marshmallow roasting. One tree had a low branch that fanned out into smaller limbs just right for

173

our purpose, but it was just a few inches higher than we could reach. No problem. I volunteered to jump up and grab the main branch and weight it down, low enough for my companions to do their duty.

Remember that the Mississippi River sometimes fluctuates forty feet within a year. During some prior high water, a fisherman had strung a nylon trotline across this particular branch. It was still there, the hook a little rusty perhaps, but the nylon line just as sturdy as ever, and at least two-hundred-pound test.

When I leaped and grabbed the branch, the hook sank up to the shank in the palm of my hand. I tried to let go, but could only do so with my left hand, leaving 180 pounds dangling from the trotline hook in my right palm. I squealed like a stuck hog, but Ed and Chief were busy gathering branches for the ladies. "Here's a good one....Oh, get that forked one for Jane, Ed..."

Sparing the gory details, let's just say the palm gave way before the hook and line. The bass section finally cut down the trotline and rushed me to a hospital forty miles away, where Dr. John, an old hunting buddy, put me back together.

So if you're going trotlining for catfish, please either gather your lines up, or use cotton so it will rot. Just for your Uncle Bob's sake.

Ed and Chief did get plenty of roasting sticks, by the way.

the "Admiral"

WHEN THE CAMELS ARE WALKING, GO TO THE BEACH

The rod arched suddenly, the reel whined as line peeled off, and Cap'n Sonny Young throttled back THE HAINT's engine. "Grab it and stick 'im!" he bellowed. Apparently fishermen in Florida were also familiar with the famous McElwee Hoist.

I did as instructed, but the king mackerel on the other end had heard, too; he, in turn, put The Hoist on me! I slid toward the stern on the wet deck, wishing that I had followed my instincts and strapped on my knee brace earlier. Now, it was too late. Grunting and straining, I slowed the fish and began regaining some line. Finally, the king surfaced momentarily behind THE HAINT. "Aw, bring 'im on in, son!" the skipper cried, "He ain't even a big one!"

Any fisherman should know certain basic rules when he goes to engage a charter captain for deep-sea fishing.

Rule Number 1: Always choose a captain who brags on your fish, no matter what size it is.

Turned out that the king was foul-hooked in the belly, and therefore tougher to boat, since I was reeling him in sideways against some eight miles of the Gulf of Mexico.

A combination business trip and speaking engagement to Mexico Beach, Florida, had included an invitation to try some of that area's fall fishing with several of the town's charter boat captains. Though it was the "off season" for tourism, it was certainly the "on season" for the fish. Over the years, these captains have cooperatively created their own fishing grounds by building artificial reefs from scuttled ships, condemned railroad bridges, and especially, junked automobiles.

Cap'n Bobby Guilford checks out these fish-attracting reefs on occasional scuba diving trips. I declined his invitation to try that, having seen the movie *Jaws*. It had been two years after that before I could work up the courage to take a bath instead of a shower. Cap'n Bobby chuckled, "Man, you should have seen me a couple of weeks ago, then. I speared a 320-pound grouper in an old school bus body. If the windshield hadn't busted out, I'd never have gotten 'im outa there!"

Rule Number 2: Choose a captain who is sane. Only a crazy man would get into a school bus with a fish twice as big as he is.

After we had gaffed my king mackerel, Cap'n Sonny had barely picked up to trolling speed again, when the second rod bent double. "Grab it and stick 'im, honey!" was the command from the bridge. Betsy leaped to comply, and was quickly linked to another king by about fifty yards of line. She stuck him several times, and began reeling. Hers came in a lot faster than mine had. Cap'n Sonny tickled him with the gaff the first time, and Betsy had to fight the fish back in, but the second swipe with the gaff was successful and the mackerel flopped on the deck. "He's about twice as big as yours!" the captain said to me.

Rule Number 3: Choose a captain who is a good judge of a fish's size.

After boating several kings and small sharks from THE HAINT, we were hailed by THE CHARISMA, a larger craft. "We're going further out to bottom fish," Cap'n Chuck Guilford allowed over the radio, "Y'all want to throw in with us for a few hours?" Since THE HAINT was a little small to venture out to the deeper water in the present sea conditions, Cap'n Sonny suggested that we accompany his colleague. It was a good decision.

On a reef formed by the old railroad trestle, which had been dismantled after its condemnation and barged out to its final resting place, we tied into schools of triggerfish and red snapper. Several times, all four of us had fish on at the same time, and Cap'n Bobby, who was crewing that day on his brother's boat, couldn't resist casting a line himself, in between taking Betsy's catches off. The action was fast and furious, but finally Cap'n Chuck called a halt. "We've got enough for our limits; let's leave some for tomorrow," he announced.

"How many is the limit?" I asked.

"Well, you didn't quite get there, but Betsy helped you out." Cap'n Chuck replied. "That gal caught more'n anybody!"

Rule Number 4: Choose a captain that can count.

That night was a town gathering and fish fry, and one of the prominent citizens asked how I did fishing. I was fixing to tell him when Cap'ns Sonny, Chuck, and Bobby chimed in: "His wife caught the biggest"; "His wife caught the most"; "His wife caught more varieties than anybody else!"

Rule Number 5: Choose a captain that can keep his mouth shut!

The next morning we rolled out well before daybreak, and met Cap'ns Bobby and Chuck for breakfast at a small cafe on the beach. As dawn began to redden the sky, Chuck stepped outside for a moment, and returned with a shake of his head. "No fishing this morning, folks," he announced. "The camels are walking."

Several American flags were visible in the dawn's early light, and they were all standing straight out, flapping in a brisk northeast wind off the backside of a huge Atlantic hurricane. "See how the horizon isn't flat, like it was yesterday?" Chuck pointed. "When you can see the humps on the horizon, you know better than to get out of port. Looks like a parade of camels, 'way out there!"

Bobby Guilford volunteered to spend the morning showing us around the area. My concept of the Florida coastline was of one long continuous line of high-rise hotels and condominiums linked by fast-food chains and wriggling like anthills with automobiles and beach bunnies. But we had run out of that type civilization almost an hour before we found Mexico Beach. Here, the pace was slower, just like small-town living in Mississippi. Folks were friendly, and took time to "pass th' time-a day."

I had also been under the impression that most of Florida spoke either Spanish, or English with a yankee accent. I heard no Spanish in three days, and the only yankee who admitted it was Eric, who owned the Toucan restaurant—"You Can

Too At Toucan's"—and if those steamed shrimp and crabs are his concoction, then we ought to allow him citizenship. He didn't say much, anyway.

Twenty minutes out of town in Bobby's four-wheel-drive pickup, we were into the boondocks: no high-rises, only an occasional house, just beach on one side and scrubby pines on the other. "Best scallops in the world come outa that bay right there," our guide pointed. There went another wrong impression: I had always thought that scallops were cut out of shark fin and manta ray with cookie cutters. "Lisa loves to snorkle for them," Bobby said, deferring to his blonde better half, who proceeded to instruct us on scalloping. Seems they come in shells, the real ones.

Money Creek was supposed to be the place where pirates had buried a treasure, "but no one's ever found any of it." However, an occasional Piece of Eight turns up on a nearby beach once in a while, according to rumors. Having said this, our driver turned his pickup off the road and drove down the beach close to the water's edge. "You have to have a permit to do this," he warned.

We drove for miles, stopping whenever the urge hit us. We walked on the sand, waded in the surf, took pictures of more pelicans than I had ever seen sitting in one place at one time (yeah, country boy Neill had to flush them!), picked up shells, or just sat on the beach and talked.

The best time to be on a beach is not when it is covered with glistening, supple, nubile bodies under a burning sun. The best time to be on a beach is when it is deserted; when the only noise is the gentle crash and roar of the breakers; when the faint salty spray collects on your lips so subtly that you don't know it's there until you lick; when

the only tracks in the sand are yours; when the little ghost crabs give you slightly startled looks as they scuttle from the water toward their holes.

Perhaps a crowded summer beach is the ideal in teenage years, but in one's forties, a lonely beach on a cloudy, windy October day is a fine place for meditation.

One of the girls found a huge conch shell, and then Bobby drove us to a spit of sand literally covered with shells of all shapes, colors, and sizes. The girls grabbed a couple of buckets and hurried off in search of treasures while Bobby and I strolled across to a little neck where a pair of men were hauling in a net. They were the only other humans in sight for miles either way. Their yellow Labrador approached to lick my hand as Bobby asked, "Y'all doing any good?"

One of the men paused and grinned at us. "Naw," he drawled, "but ain't it nice out here today?"

Well, it really was, we agreed.

When the camels are walking, go to the beach.

Betsy

ALARMING SITUATIONS

Most of us who hunt and fish will agree that we have had lots of luck nearly every time of day. I've undoubtedly bagged more turkeys and deer around nine a.m. than other times, and noon has also been a highly productive period. The best bass catch I ever saw was when Dude and I mopped up about three p.m. in the Alligator Hole; and Big Robert and Jody caught eight pounders within minutes of each other at eight-thirty a.m. Dove and quail are afternoon sports, as well as rabbit. Squirrel might be an exception, but a late evening hunt for bushytails can be fine.

So why, as Betsy loves to point out, do outdoorsmen have to get up so early in the first place?

Because the alarm clock always seems to ring an hour before dawn, is the most common answer. As to who sets it that early, well, that's a mystery.

Brother Beau used to keep the clock next to his bed, yet was always the most hostile to the shrill ringing in the pre-dawn darkness. Unless someone beat the clock getting up and punched the off button at the first jingle, it was curtains for that particular clock. Perhaps in your hunting camp, there's a civilized person who quite deliberately picks up the ringing clock and punches it off;

but the Beau Neill Method for silencing alarms tends to be rather permanent.

Using this method, one rolls over quickly in his sleeping bag and aims powerful swats in the direction of the awful ringing. Sooner or later a blow strikes the offending noisemaker, and the machine is hurled across the room, fetching up against walls, bedposts, other awakening heads, and once, clean out the door. If you plan on a five-day hunting trip with the younger Neill brother, better pack five alarm clocks.

We once tried moving the clock across the room out of his reach, but that was a mistake: it simply increased his range. He came through the darkness swinging like the Angel of Death, except more than firstborn sons felt his wrath. Before it was over he had spilled water glasses, ashtrays, flashlights, and a tacklebox full of treblehook lures across the floor before he killed the alarm. Nobody dared set foot out of bed until they could see where they were walking.

I once had a college roommate who shared the same hatred of early morning noises. Doug would roll out of the top bunk, swat the clock across the room, and then get mad at me when he'd miss his eight o'clock class. I finally cured him. I had observed that when he rolled out of bed, his foot always hit right on the same corner of the desk every time. One night after he had begun snoring, I went outside and emptied a metal garbage can. After rinsing it out, I brought it in the room and laid it on its side on top of the chest of drawers, which stood opposite the bunks. I felt sure that by placing the alarm inside the metal can, I could get much more amplification that next morning.

Then I moved the desk a mere six inches more away from the bed.

When the alarm went off the next morning, it was loud enough to wake the entire three floors of Mayes Hall. Doug was understandably more frantic than usual when he rolled off the top bunk and stepped for the desk.

Which was no longer there.

As far as I know, Doug doesn't hunt, so he will probably never read this. However, if he somehow does find out now that I moved the desk that day, surely he'll be too mature to seek revenge after thirty years. There was no permanent damage.

Speaking of alarms, I shudder to remember how a onetime hunting and fishing companion

184

once found a surefire method for waking me up and keeping me awake. We had gotten to the camp a couple of hours before dark, intending to catch a quick mess of fish for supper. However, the rain set in ten minutes before we reached the cabin. After a glum meal of canned chili and pork-'n-beans, we retired to the bunks on the screened-in back porch, vowing to try the bass during the night if the rain ended and the moon came out. The porch had a clear fiberglass roof, and my buddy had the top bunk.

Along about two a.m. I was awakened by a shake from above. My partner leaned over the side of his bed and mumbled, "The moon's out, darling." Then he rolled back over, sound asleep.

Boooiiinnnggg!!! My eyelids couldn't have opened wider had I used toothpicks. "Darling?" For the rest of that night, I lay there terrified (and this was before AIDS!) and watched that top bunk for signs of threatening movement. The next morning, he claimed no knowledge whatsoever of the incident, and even accused me of making the whole thing up. But I needed no alarm clock that day, I can sure tell you! And we didn't night fish, either.

As we grow older, many of us develop instincts to help us beat the clock, so to speak. Often I will awaken just a couple of minutes before the alarm is to ring, and can switch off the clock before it disturbs anyone else. Maybe this ability has just grown out of a desire to save clocks from Beau; maybe it's a subconscious move to treat everyone else to a hot cup of my coffee in bed; I don't know. But I can definitely say that it helps keep peace in the household if you are at home with your wife instead of at camp with the men. Betsy's not

185

partial to getting up early, so if I beat the alarm, I score points.

Yet sometimes you trust your instincts and are mistaken. Micky and I recently planned a turkey hunt for the next morning, and were going to have to rise at three to make the hour's drive to the turkey woods. We turned in rather late after a good VCR movie, with me promising to get him up with a cup of hot coffee, since I had the alarm. As usual, the metallic jangle came far too quickly after retiring; I reached over to cut off the alarm, and walked to the kitchen to light a fire under the coffee water. I was dressed by the time the water boiled, and coffee was ready two minutes later. Ever the gentleman, I took a cup of the rich brew to wake up Micky in the guest room.

He was harder to arouse than usual, and I noticed he gave me a queer look after glancing at his watch. However, he accepted the cup reluctantly and I left the room.

I was back in my room looking for a pair of socks when the metallic jangling began again. I quickly grabbed the clock, certain that I had cut it off the first time, and indeed I had. Yet the noise continued, and I finally noticed the hands were signaling 1:17. What was happening?

Then I realized that the alarming noise wasn't even coming from the clock I held. It came from a corner of the room. There I discovered the culprit: a mouse had fallen into the metal wastebasket, and was running around, frantically jumping as high as he could trying to escape. A mouse in a metal wastebasket sounds remarkably like a good alarm clock.

Micky really did look funny this time, when I walked into the guest room, took his coffee away, and told him to go back to bed and sleep two more hours.

The mouse? Oh, I taught him to swim. When it looked like he had mastered the necessary top-water skills, I pushed the little handle and let him try it underwater.

Next time we went turkey hunting, Micky insisted on keeping the alarm clock!

LEARN TO USE
ALL YOUR SENSES!

Most human hunters rely on only two of their six senses in the pursuit of game: seeing and hearing. While these two are undoubtedly the most important senses, we mortals have others, and we should learn to use and trust all the advantages at our disposal.

Actually, the two major senses are not atall infallible. How many times have you been in the woods deer or turkey hunting during the early dawn moments or that last half-hour of the day, when every stump and clump seemingly begins to move? I have on several occasions witnessed sober and otherwise sane turkey hunters fire at stumps— heck, I've even done it once. I hit what I was looking at, but what I was looking at wasn't what I thought I was looking at, even though I had been looking at it for nearly an hour.

There was one morning when I was blinded in three ridges back behind Dub's House, and had two big gobblers, from the sound of them, coming from the Blue Hole to my left. They were just over a hundred yards away, still out of sight, when a smaller turkey appeared from the draw to my right, coming straight to my calls. "Dadgum jake," I muttered, and shut up, hoping he hadn't pinpointed me.

But the turkey came steadily on. And a funny-looking short thick beard swung from its breast, at an unusual angle. The gobblers to my left sounded off again, and I gritted my teeth. Would they get within range before this little bird discovered me and spooked them?

Nope. They were gobbling their fool heads off at seventy-five yards when the jake—well, it looked like a hen, except for that short thick beard— actually poked its head in my blind. I could have grabbed it; probably should have. It said "PUTT!" and reversed direction. The two big birds shut up in mid-gobble.

Normally, I'd have let it go. But in a way, it was revenge. And "A bird in the hand is worth two in the bush," I muttered as I pulled the trigger.

It was not a jake. At some point in the little turkey's life, a wolf or bobcat had obviously jumped it, gripping it by the neck in toothed jaws. A section of skin the size of a hand had been torn out, leaving windpipe and jugular exposed. It had healed under some translucent scar tissue, and a lump of skin and feathers hung down from the wound, swinging exactly like a short thick beard. The turkey had been within two feet, and I had not seen it for what it truly was.

I was Officer of the Deck on a carrier outbound from Norfolk one winter day, and we were approaching the Gulf Stream when the starboard lookout reported a "Ship off the bow, sir, bearing 010." Before I could train my binoculars, he added, "It's upside down, sir...and huge!" The Junior OOD and the Navigator both raised their glasses, too. I stepped to the radar repeater. The only thing on the scope was a ship at twenty-seven miles, much too far to be seen with the naked eye.

But the lookout was telling the truth as he saw it. As we all focused on the bearing, sure enough, there was a ship. It was a tremendous ship, even at that distance; and it was definitely upside down!

Commander Patterson, the Navigator, was the closest man to an "old sea dog" that I've ever known. He had been a mustang (came up through the ranks) and spoke in a gravelly voice, a result of youthful boxing injuries. The poop was that he had been champ of his weight division in the Navy. He let us speculate with a knowing grin. The huge, upside down ship got even bigger, and as it grew, it also rose. Soon we could see the masts and stacks; a ship was sailing upside down, completely out of the water? I was ready to call the skipper, and the ship's doctor.

"Wait," the Navigator ordered. "You see anything at that range on radar?" We had already discussed that, and the answer was no. "Okay, then there's another explanation, right?" The older sailor was teaching here. "See that thin black line just above the horizon that merges with the ship's hull?" We did. "That's a mirror. We're seeing a reflection of that ship just over the horizon. Where the warm water of the Gulf Stream meets the cold Atlantic, sometimes it actually puts up a vapor, which the sun reflects from. And magnifies. Now watch; soon that image will disappear entirely, when the angle changes from our approaching." The words weren't out of his mouth good before the starboard lookout reported that the mystery ship was no longer there.

Fifteen minutes later, the lookout reported a ship hull down on the same bearing, but "regular size and right side up." The ship on radar was now twenty-one miles, normal sighting range on a clear day.

We had not seen what we thought we had.

The sense of sound is too often taken for granted by those who hear well. Many of us do not, so seldom depend on it. Being more or less deaf in one ear, and not hearing well out of the other, I am continually amazed at the number of turkey hunters who won't even go to the woods if they don't hear a gobble. I have (this is the lead-pipe truth!) fired over a thousand shotgun rounds at wild turkeys in my lifetime; only a couple of those turkeys have been over forty-five yards away (and I killed one of them); and I never heard a peep out of at least eighty percent of those birds. If I had to depend on hearing a gobble to hunt turkeys, I'd never hunt them.

And I've learned not to try to bluff it, either. I was at Johnny Keesee's club one spring when he and I motored down the lake and went into the woods together. In the darkness, we walked a couple hundred yards to a small clearing, where we stopped to apply camo grease and skeeter scoot, then hooted. At the second hoot, Johnny harkened: "Hear that?"

What am I going to do, admit I can't hear a turkey gobble? "Yeah!" I exclaimed.

My companion suddenly cocked his head at a different angle. "There's another one." I ain't heard nothing yet.

"Which one you want?" he asked, gathering his gear.

"Which one you want?" I countered, ever the gentleman.

Johnny nodded into the darkness, "I'll take this one. Good luck!" He strode away, leaving me with no idea where the other gobbler might be.

Pride only goes so far. "Wait, Johnny," I cried. He turned, frowning at my delay. "Point which way you think that other bird is, and how far."

Keesee points good. At seven-thirty a.m., two big gobblers walked down the ridge and up to my blind.

As usual, I missed.

The third major sense is the sense of smell, and I am convinced that many outdoorsmen don't utilize their noses as much as they should. Maybe those of us who lack in the two main senses make up for it by developing others to a greater degree. I swear that I can, and have, smelled deer and turkeys before I've seen them. Obviously, they must be close for that to happen, but in the swampland thickets and canebrakes, close counts. And of course, any Southerner knows there's a moccasin around when he suddenly gets a whiff of ripe watermelon where there ain't no ripe watermelons! Most fishermen have smelled bream beds, too. Learn to use this sense to your advantage.

One morning Adam and I were turkey hunting together—we do that a lot; he can hear and I can see colors—down by the old mill. We had blinded in and were sitting against the root ball of a blown-down hackberry, with the trunk between us. I had been calling with no response for an hour when suddenly I smelled turkey. I eased the safety off and cut my eyes right, just as a jake stepped around the root ball, less than a foot away. I never even had a chance to warn Adam; it was shoot or not.

I shot. True, that time.

What do they smell like? Well, it's a little like a barnyard odor. Next time you draw a turkey, and have washed most of the blood off your hands in a mud puddle, wait until your hands have dried and sniff them. Remember that smell. Also, a buck deer in rut has a strong musky, urine whang, and I've detected that from more than fifty yards downwind.

The sense of touch is not recommended by most authorities as a primary tool for target identification. Yet it cannot be dismissed entirely. For instance, if you reach down and touch something in your turkey blind and it is either warm and furry or cold and scaly, it's a signal that you need to change blinds, fast! And usually skivvies, as well.

There was one instance when sense of touch could have helped a hunter bag a turkey that got away, though. When Beau was young and a beginning hunter, we were together on Montgomery Island, and I had roosted a big gobbler that evening. The next morning, I gave him implicit instructions—even drew a map—as to where the turkey was. All he had to do was ease up that draw to the big split sycamore, blind in well, and call.

I was close enough to tell that he was working the bird okay, for the turkey must have gobbled fifty times. Sounded like he went straight to the sycamore, stayed there a while, then walked on off toward the sand dike, still gobbling. Yet there was no shot. We met at the Ghost, and I asked, "What happened?"

"I couldn't get a shot!" my brother wailed. "He was only two feet away, but I couldn't see to shoot!"

When Beau builds a blind, it's just that. He was invisible to the turkey, but that's a two-way street. Neither could he see the bird. "How'd you know he was two feet away, then?" I asked.

"I could see his feet, beneath the paw-paw branches! He was right beside the blind. I'd recognize those spurs again anywhere!" the young hunter asserted. "They were long and sharp, and that's the reason I didn't reach out and grab them," he headed off my question before I asked it.

It's true that the sense of taste is not a very good way to detect your prey in the woods, but for many of us, it's a major incentive to go after said prey. Once one has tasted wild turkey slow-smoked over sassafras coals, or venison loin marinated in soy sauce and lightly introduced to a fire, or beer-battered fried crappie fillets, or shish-ka-bob rabbit with mint sauce, or fried quail on toast with dewberry jelly, or barbequed bass, or broiled doves in sherry, or...hey, I'm fixing to do a cookbook!

And then there's that sixth sense: the sudden awareness that someone or something is there, watching you. In jungle warfare one is taught to avoid eye contact even when well concealed, because an alert enemy may well detect your presence by this strange, unexplainable, sixth sense. Now be honest: is any sport closer to actual combat than turkey hunting? One thing's for sure: if they gave turkeys guns, most of us would not hunt turkeys!

The best illustration I ever felt of sixth sense was not from hunting, but it was by the woods. I had left my destroyer in Charleston, headed for Mississippi and a beautiful girl, at midnight. I stood the twenty to twenty-four hundred quarter-deck watch, then signed out, throwing my already-packed bags into the white Olds 98 convertible Mountain Willy called his "Great White Bird." My cousin was deployed on a Med cruise, and had left me his car. Around three-thirty a.m. I was cruising out of a little town in eastern South Carolina, Branchville, bound for home and family. Fast.

As I came around a wooded curve, top down, radio playing, doing probably seventy-five, I heard—no, not heard so much as felt, really—a single spoken word : "Help." Not even an exclamation. Just a statement.

There's no way I could have heard a simply spoken word under those conditions, but the impression was so strong that I slowed, turned the Great White Bird around, and cruised by the curve again, radio off and eyes straining. Nothing. I went almost into town, turned again, and let the hammer down for Mississippi. Yet I was alert as I approached the curve. Suddenly, there it was again; a whisper, almost hoarse, "Help me." And then the headlight caught the movement of a hand on the side of the road, more like the flutter of a leaf in a slight breeze.

I don't remember who he was; a kid, barely younger than myself, whose car had flipped off the highway and out into the swamp. The wrecked vehicle was completely out of sight, yet the kid had dragged his broken body back to the road, and then somehow—sixth sense—made a passerby aware of his presence.

Hey, I was there. Believe it. The guy lived as a result.

So when you're in the woods, calling in your turkey blind or watching from your deer stand, and you've heard nothing, seen nothing, smelled nothing; yet just as surely as you know your name, you suddenly *know* something is there. Trust your senses. Get ready.

Of course, it might be Bigfoot.

Big Robert

Micky

THINGS TO BE SCARED OF
IN YOUR TRAVELS

Back during my farming days, I became rather insular in my outlook. Especially when the hard times hit. I didn't want to go anywhere or see anybody, and didn't want strangers coming around here. However, authors (at least authors who care about selling their books) have to make a certain amount of personal appearances, and when the storytelling facet of my career opened up, the handwriting was on the wall: I had to travel.

I held it down to places I could drive to for awhile, until Betsy found out that I was turning down exotic engagements that involved getting on airplanes. Paying exotic engagements. More handwriting went on the wall: I had to fly in an airplane.

There are a lot of people in the world today that are afraid to fly in airplanes, of which I am one. I have tried to analyze my fear, coming to the conclusion that I am not necessarily scared of the actual flying, but of turning control of my life over to some stranger who just happens to drive airplanes for a living. The popular view of pilots when I was coming along was that of a guy who drank and chased women all night. Some were even said to be yankees.

Betsy booked me onto this airplane flying out of New Orleans (is that a heaven for the above-described pilots, or what?) and contracted with Ted Daly and Admiral Drake to make sure I got on the durn thing. I was working up a major-league pucker factor. Bear in mind that except for a few low-level flights with our crop-duster—trusted friend David Steen—I had not flown since the service and choppers. There really needs to be someone on the ground with a gun to encourage me to board an airplane. The pilot looked barely old enough to shave, and none of the stewardesses were even remotely pretty. Matter of fact, one of them was male; this wasn't going to be atall like the television commercials.

The flight out was at night, because of several delays, and I did learn one thing almost immediately upon takeoff, though it wasn't the kind of knowledge you'd brag on. It was, bad ears are infinitely worse in big airplanes than on crop-dusters or helicopters. Since my fear ratio was about the same in all three cases, I guess ear pain is altitude. Then there was some kind of trouble with the engine during our layover in Houston. After an hour of trying to fix it, they declared that our vehicle was deceased, and offloaded everyone to change planes. I learned that *real* courage is getting onto a second airplane after they tell you that the first one was broke.

By the time we got fixed up with another plane, it was past suppertime, but they passed out coke (liquid) and nuts to us nuts who had decided to press on. Soon we were up and flying over Texas and New Mexico, and after a while, I pulled back the little window shade to see what I could see. Not much, except for what appeared to be a small airfield: bright red and white beacons shining in the blackness. I shut the curtain.

A little while later, I looked out again. By golly, the same airfield was in the same position out there, unless it was a regularlyappearing line of beacons for night flights. I pulled the shade to ponder on this, but not for long. In just a couple of minutes, I peeked out again. The field was in the same place. I jerked the curtain shut to think this over.

Obviously, we had been circling the airfield for an hour in the night, which meant we had problems of some kind. Maybe we were using up or dumping fuel before a crash landing? Some damn terrorist had invaded the cockpit and had us landing on a rinky-dink, little, too-short strip in Mexico? The pilots had gone to sleep and left the automatic pilot in turn-signal mode? Not wanting to alarm the rest of the mostly-sleeping passengers, I casually beckoned the stewardess over.

"Ma'am, do we have some kind of troubles?" I whispered.

She shook her head and smiled. "No, why?"

"Well, we seem to have been circling that little airfield down there for an awful long time now," I pointed out.

"What airfield?" she demanded, and leaned across to the window. Obligingly, I pulled the shade and pointed out the red and white beacons in the darkness.

"That airfield!" I said rather harshly, thinking that there should be some regulation that they have to tell the passengers about emergencies. After all, we need to make final plans too.

Her smile became a smirk. "Sir, many years ago, we installed *wing lights* on all our aircraft! Can I get you a drink?"

The bad thing was, she was also on the flight back.

So it's no secret that I prefer to drive if I have to go somewhere, yet there are dangers involved in highway travel, too. Real danger, lurking and skulking around constantly, so as to maliciously and vindictively attack me to cause pain, suffering, and embarrassment. One must be ever vigilant, and ready to be terrified at a moment's notice.

I let my guard down one time, and left the window down on the van to boot. It had been a late night before, so I was rather bleary-eyed as I poured my fourth cup of coffee and went to town to get the mail. Hotted it up pretty good in the microwave right before I left the house. I was tooling along sipping coffee, not thinking about anything in particular, when all of a sudden this cat lands right in my lap!

I had known that China was expecting, but had never even considered that she might pick the van to have her kittens in.

Well, we didn't wreck, but I'm not sure that a mild ditching isn't preferable to hot coffee in your lap. Thank goodness the cat took about half the coffee—which she certainly deserved. Things could have been a lot worse for me had she not been situated exactly where she was, lapwise, and anyway her hair grew back rather quickly. Still, I had to think long and hard about Betsy's possible reaction before deciding that the kittens didn't deserve to be orphaned.

Ever since that time I've been a little more attuned to any foreign presences in automobiles. I cast an eye about before I get in, and I try to be aware of hostile wavelengths. After a lapful of hot coffee, one tends to develop seventh and eighth senses, not to mention sixths.

One day I headed out in the van, and was probably five miles from home when I sensed that there was Something There. Even more disturbing, it was a Hostile Presence. Don't ask me how I knew; I just did. Without stopping (this was my second mistake; my first was a less-than-thorough search before embarkation) I began to cut my eyes around the van to check it out. Nothing. I searched in the rearview mirror for Presences behind me, remembering a picture show about a alien hand with long dripping hypodermic finger-nails that got into a young couple's car. As far as I could tell, there were no venom-filled hypodermics back there; I even felt gingerly behind my seat for a Presence's hand.

I concentrated, tuning in on the ominous radi-ations emanating from somewhere close. Still squinting and focusing, I turned a corner, heading into the sun. Automatically, I reached up and pulled down the sun visor.

A wasp was building a nest on the inside of the visor. A red wasp. One of those big ole mean red wasps; the kind that hunts down helpless young tender orphans and stings them, just for the fun of it.

In a van, there ain't much room between your head and the sun visor.

I have never been charged by a man-eating lion, nor a rogue elephant. I don't need to be. There is more Pure-D Nasty rolled up into one big ole mean red wasp than every man-eating lion in Africa. Give me a rogue elephant behind my sun visor any day, in preference to a big ole mean man-eating red wasp.

A lot transpired in the next few seconds, and I hope the lady who was meeting me at the time reads this, so she'll know what happened. Just before we passed, I opened the door and stepped to the running board to jump from my speeding van; never mind that the lady in the approaching car was almost even with my front bumper. At the same time, the wasp charged, and the swoosh of wind from the suddenly opened door sucked him out, narrowly missing my head. As the wasp went by, I rethought my policies on jumping into the path of speeding automobiles from other speeding automobiles, especially now that the wasp was outside. I re-entered the van and slammed the door just before the lady creamed it. We careened safely past each other, by the hardest.

I apologize, Ma'am, and hope you understand now.

I do hate wasps.

Some fellow travelling outdoorsmen are not as readily terrorized by wasps and airplanes as I am, perhaps, but then they have their own problems. As in Jim's case.

This was an outdoor writer friend, one of those big macho guys who wrestle alligators, catch big poisonous snakes, and stick their heads into lion's mouths, when alligators, snakes, and lions are available and will hold still for such treatment. It's Jim's story, and I give him full credit for it; you don't catch me doing such things.

Jim was returning from an engagement in the Carolinas, it seems, when he rounded one of those mountain curves and spied a four-foot-long copperhead wriggling along the side of the road, minding its own business. The scribe braked and pulled over to observe the serpent, four-foot copperheads being unusual any-where. This one seemed even a little longer than that, once Jim approached on foot, and then the idea struck our hero: why not catch the snake and take it home? Told you it wasn't me.

Once he had the reptile in hand, he remembered that a good snake-catcher always secures his snake-container before securing the snake. Poor timing, but he had to make the best of it now. A four-foot copperhead is not as easy to turn loose as one might suppose. Finding no container readily at hand, he fumbled into his pocket (with the hand holding the tail, of course), got his keys out, and unlocked the small foreign car's trunk. There was nothing in there, so he simply dumped his captive in and slammed the lid. Nothing to it.

A couple of hours down the road, Jim pulled into a station to gas up, and decided to check on his new pet. He carefully opened the trunk. It was empty.

There was no sign of the snake; and a four-foot copperhead is easily noticeable, believe me. It took real courage for our hero to stick his head into the space and look in all the little nooks and crannies. No snake.

Normally, it doesn't take long to get a spare tire out of that hole in the trunk under the carpeting. But when one is convinced that an angry poisonous snake is in there with the tire, it can take quite a while. The station attendant made the writer pull his little car away from the pump area when it was revealed to the curious onlookers what the problem was, and the gathering crowd backed off a bit.

When the spare tire well was finally emptied, it exposed no spare reptiles. At this point, Jim grasped the edge of the trunk carpet and ripped the covering completely out of the vehicle, a job totally unsuited for weaker men. Fear, adrenalin, and exasperation can work wonders, however. Still, no snake was revealed. Only the back of the car's back seat.

Our writer confesses to being a pretty fair shade-tree mechanic; it would usually only take him a half-hour to remove the seats from his vehicle. In this case, however, it required nearly three hours, using looonnngg wrenches borrowed from the station attendant. Once again, no snake. The interior carpeting did not tear out quite as readily as the trunk's did, but it too eventually joined the growing stack of material to the side of the stripped car. There wasn't a copperhead under the rug.

Now one could see all the way from the trunk to the dashboard, and no snakes were visible. Jim could not pay any of the onlookers enough to slide into the car upside down and investigate the underside of the dashboard. Knowing there were few places left large enough to conceal a four-foot copperhead, he fatalistically did so himself. Nope, no snakes in the wiring.

They checked the engine itself, as the last hideout. Nada.

Reluctantly, Jim began to replace furnishings, in the knowledge that he was probably going to have to take them out again soon.

Only what was required to motivate down the highway was bolted down; the rest was shoved into the trunk. Finally, almost five hours after he had pulled in for gas, our hero drove away from the station, sitting on the edge of his seat and glancing around the interior more than down the road itself.

Fifteen minutes later on the interstate, the seat belt (one can understand why the driver wasn't buckled up), which had somehow been stretched out under the seat during reassembly, came free and zipped by Jim's britches leg as the spring rewound.

No, the car was not totalled. But it was sold, and soon. There are few things worse than seeing a large poisonous snake in close proximity, but one of those things is *not* seeing a large poisonous snake when you know durn well he's somewhere close!

Haven't bought a small, used, foreign car lately, have you?

While I have a healthy respect for snakes, they don't scare me nearly as much as airplanes, wasps, and certain critters that are known to be out there lurking in the darkness. Things like—verevolfs and wampires!

When we hosted our Viking foreign exchange student for a year awhile back, though that wasn't particularly scary, it did adversely affect our speech on a permanent basis. Now, Johan says "ain't" and "y'all" and we say "velcome," "Wolksvagen," or "Wolwo." And "wampire" and "verevolf."

I don't watch scary movies, simply because they scare me, even if I cover my eyes during the bloody parts. If for some stupid reason I do slip up and view some horrible being performing unspeakable acts on half the human population of Rolling Fork, I don't sleep without the lights or Betsy for a week.

The only possible exception is an occasional wampire flick. In advertisements and previews, I have observed that wampires seem to prefer scantily-clad beautiful girls for wictims, and I have found that if I watch the wictims instead of the wampires, I can sometimes muddle through the picture show. Wampires don't tend to be nearly so messy or gory as most other monsters, either. Some of them are even almost gentlemanly in their advances toward their gorgeous wictims.

But not verevolfs! Those huge mean monsters will tear your arm off and beat you about the head and shoulders with the gory end of it. It didn't take but a couple of verevolf shows for me to catch onto those guys. Stay away from verevolfs!

What's bad is when the previews lead you to believe it's a wampire flick, and then they mix in some verevolfs and zombies and ghouls, who not only scare the p-wadding out of you, but go to ripping up the beautiful wictims! At least the wampires are civilized about their feeding habits; what good is a hobgoblin who picks on a lissome blonde instead of a defensive tackle? Come to think of it, I've seen defensive tackles that would make most verevolfs look like sissies!

I was on a business trip, and the hotel television movie was advertised as a wampire story, with a swimming pool setting; you know, bikinis and all that. It beat an hour news program and a wrestling match, on the other channels, all hollow. Started off good, too. But then, before I had time to close my eyes, a mixed pack of red-eyed verevolfs and wampires charged out of the trees and turned the swimming party into a dissecting session, with more howls and blood than Channel 2's wrestling match! The fiends faded back into the woods, chuckling evilly, their red eyes glowing in the darkness. I quickly cut off the television.

In the middle of the night, I awoke suddenly, aware of another presence in the room. It's a real act of courage to open your eyes when you know a wampire is in the room. Don't try it on verevolfs; slip under the bed with your eyes still shut.

I peeked out from under squinted lids. Sure enough, two red eyes glowed in the darkness, towering over me! A nine-foot-tall wampire! I knew that with the big ones, your only chance is to take them by surprise; screeching my best Rebel Yell, I sprang to the attack, flailing, clawing, punching for my life!

In the daylight, you don't realize that those durn smoke detectors have little red lights inside of them, do you?

HUNTING FOR YOUR HUNTING CLOTHES

Warm weather hunting doesn't pose a problem for most of us nimrods; we just snag a pair of jeans and a camo tee shirt that we've been wearing off and on all summer anyway. Even bowhunting in warm weather usually requires only a camo jumpsuit that's lightweight and been worn to clean out the dog pen or cut firewood. But when old Jack Frost comes to town, we hunters have to dig out the warm stuff we put up last February.

Therefore, I start to look for my deer hunting gear when the cold and frost season arrives. After an hour or so of digging through the cedar chest, the hall closet, my closet, our closet, the dirty clothes, and the shelves under the gun cabinet, Betsy finally sat up in bed (Oh, yeah: the rule is, you never start looking for hunting stuff until ten o'clock the night before the hunt; that's in the Bible somewhere) and demanded, "What the heck are you looking for now?!"

"My red long handles," I declared. That's in the Bible, too: never admit to looking for more than one lost garment at a time. Had I told her how many things were out of pocket, she'd have accused me of being senile. (Late at night, she tends to forget that I've suffered a memory loss from Lyme Disease.)

"Oh," she mumbled, and pulled the covers back over her head. "Look in B.C.'s room."

Why a high school senior girl would want a set of red, flap-in-the-back, fourteen-button-up-the-front long johns, I wasn't sure, but I went and asked. B.C. put the phone down, reached under her bed, and produced the missing drawers. "Wore 'em to a party, with your mammoflage boxer shorts over them," she explained as she picked the phone back up. I started to ask the obvious question, but then decided I didn't want to know.

My web belt was missing from under the gun cabinet that next morning, and I had to make do by slipping my scabbard knife on my jeans belt, and extra clip in my pocket. Upon inquiry after school the next day, the same culprit produced the belt, sans all the little pouches. "A Survival Party," she explained. Further search revealed the pouches under the bed days later. The extra clip pouch was okay, but the beltpack was missing the skeeter scoot, compass, and lucky wad of toilet paper. She failed to grasp the significance of this last item even after I explained that I had had that wad so long that I knew I'd never need it as long as I had it, don't you see? The compass mysteriously appeared a day or so later. Never have found my lucky wad.

Then I couldn't find my heavy gray sweater; the one Betsy knitted for me and I got a bloodstain on the front of while showing off a wild turkey gobbler and had to convert to a hunting sweater. You guessed it: B.C. again. It's amazing how far a deer can smell "Red" perfume, isn't it? Especially a big buck. The sweater wasn't under the bed, however. It was stacked neatly in her wardrobe along with my blue one, my white one, and my green one.

Men, why is it that it's okay for daughter to wear your sweaters, but not okay for wife to find long blonde hairs on your shoulder after you retrieve your garments? There's an obvious explanation for those hairs, but it is never accepted by the womenfolks.

I missed a favorite blue stone-washed canvas hunting shirt sometime last spring. Thought I'd left it either in east Tennessee or south Mississippi after turkey hunts with friends. Called the folks I'd hunted with in both places and asked them to look. Called a lady at whose home I had changed before speaking to a banquet about that time. Called Semmes Ross, where I always stop if I have time coming through South Mississippi. Semmes has a teenage daughter, too. "Look in B.C.'s room, under the bed," he advised from two hundred miles away.

Sure enough, there it was. Along with a glove that had been missing for two years and four 30.06 cartridges. No lucky wad yet, though.

I had been aware for some time, even before the recent spate of television commercials on the subject, that there are products one can use to prevent the buildup of static electricity in one's garments. Personally, I have never seen the need for such use to prevent a nice-looking young lady's skirt from riding up. Were we in Scotland, however, I can readily see that most wives would use double doses of the best anti-static product available during the weekly kilt-washing. All depends on who's wearing the garment infected with static, obviously.

As a former cotton grower, I have to believe that most of the problem could be solved by outlawing polyester clothes. Any hunter who has ever worn polyester underwear can testify to the riding-up tendency of such skivvies, not to mention the medical complications brought on by wearing any other drawers than cotton during our Southern summer heat and humidity. When President Carter embargoed the shipment of cotton to Russia after the Reds invaded Afghanistan, his strategy was to force the dirty commies to wear polyester underwear in the Afghan heat, which would result in a raging case of jock itch for the whole Red Army. A soldier busy scratching cannot shoot accurately, so the Afghan rebels with their crossbows and muzzleloaders soon had Russia's finest begging for mercy. Ten years hence, they've torn down the Berlin Wall, declared Perestroika and Glastnost, and voted in democracy, preferring politicians to polyester underwear.

Are you beginning to understand the dangers of static cling?

I recently found that not only can static cling hurt one physically, it can ruin one's reputation as well.

My favorite shirt had been washed the day before and I went over to the dryer to get it out before heading in to the post office. Tucking in my shirttail, I decided that it wasn't cold enough for a jacket, so I drove into town enjoying the unseasonably warm weather. It got warmer when I went into the post office.

I noticed that some folks eyed me with renewed interest, but then I'm not home a lot anymore, so I put it down to just seeing old friends after a period of absence. One old high school buddy grinned and gave me a thumbs-up over raised eyebrows. A couple of church ladies seemed to cut me cold, for some strange reason. A gaggle of children on their way to school broke into giggles as I left the post office and passed them, but I assumed they were remembering something from their night's frolics. When I got back in the car, I noticed a crowd had gathered on the post office steps, and that some of the looks from the men were admiring. Was I acquiring an Author's Aura, I wondered?

Back home, as I slid out of the vehicle, something brushed the back of my neck and crackled slightly. Everyone knows how terrified I am of wasps, and that was the first thing that crossed my mind. I frantically slapped at the back of my neck.

No, it wasn't a wasp. It was static cling. Clinging to the back of my shirt, obviously since I had removed it from the dryer, was a pair of peach-colored bikini panties. The static crackled as I removed them from their perch.

No, they were not mine, nor were they cotton. The ladies in the household do not always share my views on skivvy material.

Question is, now that I think about it, at my age did this hurt, or help, my reputation?

While we're talking under our clothes here, let me reveal to the rest of the hunting world a recent discovery I made that will revolutionize the Outdoor Industry, as well as save you enough money over the next few years to burn a wet mule.

I was deer hunting the first gun season, and was rewarded for my patience in the tree stand when a seven-point buck came ambling up about eight a.m. Problem was, the deer was on the other side of a little slough that was only about ten yards wide, but about ten feet deep in the middle. As I watched, rifle up, the buck walked up to the edge of the ditch and looked across, obviously considering coming to my side. Since it was almost a half-mile back to a road across the slough, I decided to wait until he crossed before I shot.

Not to be; the deer stood at the water's edge for several minutes, then turned and started back the way he had come. I dropped him with a neck shot; he never knew I was there.

Now, however, I was faced with a choice: did I walk a half-mile to the road, cross the slough, walk a half-mile back to the buck, field-dress him, then drag him a half-mile back to the road? Or, did I want to somehow cross the slough here, swim the deer ten yards back across the water, then field-dress him and drag him only a hundred yards to the field edge I could drive to?

Hey, I'm no dummy. This was a pretty big deer, and I'm a broke-down older person. Never drag a deer a half-mile when you can drag him a hundred yards, I figured. So, all I had to do was wade out, swim a few stokes, wade to the deer, and repeat the crossing with my trophy. No problem, right?

Well, it was November. But it wasn't really *that* chilly.

I could recall the day when me and Troy and the Dixie Tixie went skinny-dipping in the Grudge Ditch in February on a dare. I could remember the December right after we finished freshman football at Ole Miss when I killed that huge ten-point on the other side of Christmas Tree Lake; I just bodaciously picked that sucker up in my arms and carried him two hundred yards through waist-deep

water to the Rim Road. I could remember when
Jerry Center and I were shooting ducks up at
Coontown and the ice broke with me and I got
buck naked on the bank of Sardis Lake in a snow-
storm while changing out of my wet clothes into
Center's dry second layer. Hell, I could remember
when I was T-U-Double-Uff Tough!

So, I stripped right down to my skivvy shorts,
leaned my rifle against a tree, and waded in.

Water gets a lot colder nowadays, what with
holes in the ozone layers and all. I noticed that
before I was knee deep. As I approached crotch
level, I began to look for icebergs. I was therefore
not reluctant to halt my forward progress when I
heard a commotion in a nearby thicket on my side
of the ditch. Spying a deer running toward me, I
quickly retraced my steps to the bank and grabbed
my rifle. Certainly I wouldn't have broken the law,
but if a fourteen-point buck had charged out of
that thicket, I wanted to be in a position to be
tempted, at least. Didn't want to get caught with
my britches down, so to speak.

It wasn't a buck, but two does, that charged
me. And they really looked like they were charging. They ran right up within ten feet of where I
stood in my skivvy shorts (regular white skivvies,
not boxers or those little Valentines Day bikini
shorts with the hearts and flowers) and stopped
without seeing me. Suddenly a pack of five wild
dogs burst out of the thicket, and the two deer
raced by close enough for me to touch. Never saw
me atall. The canines also charged straight for me,
which isn't a good feeling even if you aren't
standing there in skivvies. They seemed to look
right through me at the departing deer. Didn't see
me even when I raised my gun.

Three dogs fell to my shells remaining in the clip, but the survivors never flinched. They ran right by me in their pursuit of the deer. I grabbed my jeans and shirt, reloaded, and took out after them.

But the lesson here is perfectly clear. All those camouflage companies have been selling us a bill of goods these many years. This experience has proven to us all that naked hunters are invisible to animals in the woods. Obviously, they can't smell naked hunters either. Even goose bumps are clearly undetectable!

Oh, and I'm planning further research on it to prove that gender makes no never mind. I need a couple of lady hunters for my next trip; a blonde and a redhead. I have a brunette at home, if I can talk her into hunting with me in this manner.

I heard about an interesting variation on this theme that was initiated by the fairer sex, and it really uncovers, so to speak, some disadvantages we men have in our choice of skivvies, when they must be utilized for emergency purposes.

To better understand my point, we must go back to when Dude was coming down one afternoon to sight in his rifle.

Four o'clock came and went. No Dude. Five came and went. No Dude. I had choir practice at six, and when that time approached, I took off for town, seeing no sign of my missing buddy.

I returned to find an irate Dude. He had hit a big pothole and skidded into the ditch a little over a mile north of my house. After speaking frankly to the situation in his own inimitable style for some several minutes, which failed to resurrect the car from the ditch, he began to walk down the road toward my house. Predictably, no one came along to pick him up.

"I wasn't but a hundred yards away when you took off west for town in your pickup. I jumped up and down, waved my arms, and hollered, but you just kept right on trucking!" he declared, clearly aggravated at my snub.

"Dude, look at yourself," I replied reasonably. He was clothed from head to foot in camouflage. No wonder I had never seen him! Even his Flag of Distress was camo. He looked like a half-acre of newground, blowing in the breeze.

"Oh," was all he said.

I was visiting Ross McGehee to turkey hunt recently when a couple of Maggie's friends dropped by. Seems the two ladies had been down to New Orleans shopping, and were driving back late that afternoon when their car conked out on the

Interstate highway. After determining that they were incapable of repairing the whateveritis, they attempted to wave down some help, just as Dude had in our earlier experience. As had happened with him, no one stopped. These ladies, however, had another solution to their problem; Necessity is the Mother of Invention.

One of them stepped to the off side of the car and removed her half-slip. They tried using this garment as a Flag of Distress, but still with no results. Traffic continued to zip by at seventy-five miles per hour.

When we consider that, it's really not surprising, is it? I mean, a half-slip might just as well be a pillowcase when waved by the side of the road. There are really no distinguishing features that can be displayed to advantage; not at ten feet and seventy-five miles per hour in broad daylight, anyway.

Once the thought process had started, however, there was a natural progression. It just required a few minutes of privacy in the car itself, and then new Flags of Distress were waved. Men, we have a distinct disadvantage in the field of makeshift Flags of Distress. Suffice it to say that these ladies stopped traffic. Their vehicle was repaired free of charge, and they were graciously escorted by convoy to their exit. These were nice-looking young ladies, and they had nice-looking lingere, it is said. I now understand that there is a regular patrol of young men on that stretch of Interstate, on the lookout for Damsels In Distress.

It would not have worked with red, one-piece long handles!

And too often, I swear I'll never wear those again.

It happened again last season; I was deer hunting out in the hills, slipping down a little creek. The water was only ankle-deep on the sand bars that dotted the narrow branch, and as the stream wandered from side to side of the six-foot-high banks, so did I, stepping across on the bars when the path changed sides. I had followed this course for a couple hundred yards, and was crossing again, when the ankle-deep sandbar failed to hold me. One innocent step, and I was waist-deep!

Luckily, I had seen enough Tarzan movies in my youth to know what to do. The creek was so narrow that I could lean forward and throw my rifle sling over a root on the bank. Moments later I was standing shakily on solid ground, wet from the waist down. The temperature was about twenty-five (good old American Farenheit, not that communistic Celcius) and I was a half-mile from camp. I climbed the bank and headed for a heater, not even pausing to dump the water out of my boots.

But once in camp (where there was no change of clothes, only a gas heater) I still had a problem: I was wearing one-piece long johns, the kind with the traditional flap in the rear.

Tradition is wonderful unless you must get jaybird-naked in freezing weather to honor it. Back home in the closet were two pairs of two-piece thermal long handles which, had I been wearing them, would have only allowed half of me to be exposed to the elements. Once again, I swore (and swore off!) one-piece long johns.

I'll never forget the time that Jerry Center and I were duck hunting on Sardis Lake while we were at Ole Miss. It was blowing sleet and snow in a twenty-knot gale, and the lake was frozen for a hundred yards away from the bank. But the wind was keeping the ducks stirred up off the main lake, and the mallards were flying the lakebank in flocks, looking for sanctuary. I had on hip boots, and was breaking my way through the ice to a couple of downed drakes, when I hit a tough spot. The sheet of ice held momentarily as I stumbled, then gave way as I went to my knees. I was soaked to the waist in blizzard conditions.

I had on one-piece long johns.

I retrieved the ducks, and made my way back to the bank, where my comrade seemed more concerned that I was flaring the low-flying flocks than for my health. At that time I was playing football, and was in pretty decent physical shape; Center was playing house, and was less than 140 pounds soaking wet, a condition I now threatened him with. Though Jerry's long johns were obviously going to be too small for me, they were also obviously a lot dryer and warmer than what I was wearing. And they were two-piece. As we both stripped, I pointed out that, lucky him, he was only going to have to be exposed halfway, whereas I was going to be stark nude on the bank of Sardis Lake in a howling blizzard.

When I shucked those one-piece long johns, they stood on their own two feet. The wet bottom half froze solid instantly. My wet bottom half wasn't too far behind. Squeezing a 200-pound guard into cheerleader-size underwear leaves a lot of exposed guard, and I resolved then and there to put Center on a weight-gain program. The boy also had size eight socks, but there again, size eight dry socks beat size eleven wet socks all hollow. I dried the inside of my boots as well as I could with the tops of my long handles (which are still standing on the bank of Sardis Lake, for all I know), and would you believe we finished out our limits before we left?

That was not the first time, nor will it be the last time, that I resolve never to wear one-piece long johns again!

And there's one other type underwear I shy away from now.

Many years ago, I was the main participant in one of those wet highway skids, resulting in several broken vertebrae, a busted sternum, collapsed lungs, and the near-total destruction of the Green Scout when it was still a farm pickup. There will always be a warm place in my heart for Carl Conlee, who joined the small huddle of onlookers, took off his raincoat, and held it over me until the ambulance arrived. There's also a place for the guy who stopped on the side of the road and hollered out across the soybean field, "Is he dead yet?"

And as they loaded me into the ambulance a few minutes later, I remember thinking what most well-bred Southern young men would have thought in the same situation: "Did I wear good clean underwear this morning?"

I can recollect my grandmother discarding skivvy shorts that had just gotten to the comfortable stage, with the admonition, "You can't wear these holey things! What if you have an accident?"

Well, I had never stopped to consider that before. I mean, when they bring you into the hospital emergency room broken and bleeding, do the doctors and nurses have some sort of style show judging of their patients' undergarments? Since my grandfather was a doctor, I assumed that my grandmother must have known what she was talking about, but we never got down to specifics.

There must be something to it, though, because a few years later when I got my driver's license, one of the first things Momma drilled into me was: "Be sure you have nice clean underwear on, in case of an accident!"

And sure enough, when I got ready to leave the hospital a couple of months later, my good clean skivvies that I had worn in were nowhere to be found. If I had had my holey drawers on when I wrecked, would I have gotten them back? Is there a black market for nice clean skivvies that hospitals use to balance their budgets? Maybe there's a trophy room down in the basement next to X-ray.

What about the ladies? In thinking back, I can never remember either my mother or my grandmother warning one of the fairer sex about checking the condition of their undergarments. It must be the assumption that girls don't have accidents, for I sure recall that in our college days, such dainties were definitely considered trophies, requiring weeks of planning for a well-organized Panty Raid on the girls' dorm.

Well, whatever happens to nice clean underwear in hospitals, I'll bet that today's styles have added a little spice to the life of emergency room doctors and nurses. Why, just the other day after a rain shower, my van went into a slight skid on the wet asphalt, but fortunately I regained control. Yet the thought flashed through my mind as I fought the wheel: "Did I wear nice clean underwear this morning?"

Followed quickly by, "Oh, Lord! I think I've got on those silly bikini shorts with the little red hearts and flowers that Betsy gave me for Valentine's Day!"

OUTDOOR ISSUES
AND ANSWERS
(Or At Least,
Opinions!)

All writers are tempted at times to address issues that they feel strongly about, simply because they have a forum. And it usually doesn't make two hoots in hallelujah whether the writer's opinions are well thought-out or not, they're going to tell you what they think.

Of course, you can get the same thing with your morning coffee down at the cafe, generally without having to pay the price of a book or newspaper. It's just that if you get charged for it, you feel the guy ought to have sense enough to see it like you do, right?

Not trying to break my arm patting my back here, but to my eternal credit, the majority of my writing has been done with one thing in mind: that the reader feels better coming out than he did going in. Let the other folks do the critical, bitchy writing; Neill's makes you feel good. At least, that was what I shot for, whether I hit it or not.

But that doesn't mean I don't have strong feelings about some of the things going on nowadays, and every now and then I'll bust loose and write about it. Yet I still try to not be painful with my opinions. Try these, which originally came out as newspaper columns.

And what the heck; if you don't like the way I think, write me back. I won't charge for reading yours!

QUICK-DRAW NEILL

There was a recent hassle about some fellow in a big city who used a handgun to wound a trespasser on his property. The whole flap was rather ludicrous to the average country home-owner, for most of us believe that a man's home is his castle, and woe betide any unwelcome intruder. Many of us keep a handgun around for just such a purpose, though only on the rarest of occasions is there a need. Especially if you also own a Labrador.

Years ago, there was a rash of break-ins in our community, and a buddy of mine who was in the military overseas wrote me and asked me to teach his wife, who was still at home, how to use their pistol. I did so, glad to help out, and soon Jody was proficient with the gun. About a week later, we saw her at a party.

"Oh, I'm so glad you taught me to use that gun!" she exclaimed. "You'll never guess what happened last night!"

"You had a burglar?" I asked.

"Well, not quite. But I was awakened by a loud noise from the kitchen in the middle of the

224

night. Scared me to death!" she shuddered, recall-ing. "I was terrified the rest of the night, but in the morning I found that a mouse had knocked an empty Coke bottle off of the shelf under the sink and it landed in a dishpan. Yet I just knew it was a burglar when I heard it!"

"Did you get the pistol out of the bedside stand and go check?" I queried.

She shook her head. "No, I just pulled the covers up over my head for the rest of the night!"

It was during this same crime wave when Beau took his family on vacation and asked me to keep an eye on his house, just down the road. A couple of nights later, I noticed a light on in his den. Grabbing my pistol, I jumped in the truck and took off down the road to investigate. Sure enough, the front door was standing wide open.

(Turned out they had arranged with their maid for her to come clean that day, but they hadn't told me. The lady had not closed the door securely and it had blown open. She had also left a den lamp on. But how was I to know?)

Pistol in one hand, flashlight in the other, and pounding heart in my throat, I entered the house to confront the intruder. The old military training came back (or was it from TV cop shows?) and I went in low, light held out to the side, so if an armed burglar fired at the light he'd miss me.

No one was in the living room. I tiptoed down the hall and paused to breathe deeply before I dodged around the den door. Nothing there, except the lighted lamp. Kitchen next, then break-fast room. No one. I dried my palms on my britches leg and continued down the dark, narrow hallway. The sound of my pounding heart filled my ears; could the robber hear it, too?

Silently I opened doors on either side. The kids' bedrooms were clear. The bathroom was empty, but I couldn't help thinking of a scene from *Psycho* as I eased the shower curtain open with the pistol barrel. I wiped sweat from my brow as I prepared to enter the last bedroom. I went in low, pistol ready, light held to the side. He had to be close now.

The closet door stood wide open.

This was it: the last refuge, the Robbers Roost. Bravely I swallowed the lump in my throat, took a deep breath, and lunged low, into the doorway.

A man with a flashlight and gun crouched there! Aiming at *me*! No time for anything but reflexes! Him or me!! "*Shoot!* Shoot quick!" my mind cried.

The back of a closet is a silly place to keep a full-length mirror.

LOGIC ON THE FUR ISSUE

There has been a great deal of media hype recently on a subject that makes very little sense to most people. Therefore, acting on demand from public outcry, let's try to look at the situation cooly and logically, and put things in perspective.

There are some folks scattered about who believe that the wearing of fur is immoral, unethical, un-Christian, rude, crude, and socially unacceptable. Fine; everybody ought to believe something, I've always said. Personally, I believe onions ought to be abolished.

Just like the Fur Fighters, I stand on the strength of my convictions. I refuse to use onions when I cook, don't plant them in the garden, don't wear them, don't write on onionskin paper, pick out the pieces I find some hostess has slipped into her recipes, and don't kiss girls who order onion rings with their cheeseburgers—for at least ten minutes after eating. I never buy sour cream and onion flavored potato chips. I spray deadly chemicals on wild onions in the wheat or the yard, then chortle fiendishly as they curl up and die in agony.

However, my being against onions hardly gives me the right to go into your garden and pull up your Vidalias, does it? Not as long as my legislators have stupidly resisted my heart-rending appeals to outlaw the durn things once and for all. If it's not against the law to grow and eat onions, then you have the right to choose to do so, secure in your own ignorance. Even though your breath may shrivel your toothbrush bristles each morning.

Most Fur Fighters, however, seem to be missing the fact that fur grows from skin, and the skins are actually what folks are wearing garments made of. Some members of the sheep and goat tribe contribute their fur for garments while still retaining rights to their own skin, but minks, otters, possums, rabbits, foxes, and other popular fur-coat-contributing species are compelled to shed their whole dermis and epidermis along with the fur.

As do cattle, when leather shoes, belts, gloves, jackets, purses, and wallets are manufactured.

If I'm a Fur Fighter, and don't want to appear hypocritical about this whole tempest in a teapot, looks like I'd be honor-bound not to wear leather products either, right?   Nor should I watch the Super Bowl, or any other pigskin-kicking, catching, carrying contest. No World Series, since baseballs and mitts are made from cowhide—undoubtedly dead cowhide. Basketballs are leather, aren't they, as are most tennis shoes? Another No-No.

Feather pillows are out, as far as this hypothetical non-hypocritical Fur Fighter is concerned, as well as down coats. Down is about the same as fur, except it comes from birds—dead birds. You never see naked chickens and ducks running around, do you?   The down comes off when the poultry is prepared for the family meal, as do feathers, feet, and beaks. And skin.

So, Fellow Fur Fighters, if we're going to be against wearing skins in the good old U.S.A., what's our course of action? Logically, we go to our legislators, and attempt to convince them that they need to pass laws against making products from skin, fur, or feathers, and to outlaw other cruel things, like onion eaters. And when those laws are passed, we arrest, convict, and execute the skin-wearers and onion-eaters.

Until that time, we show the Courage of our Convictions by not using those skin-products ourselves, or eating onions.

But we don't run up and throw paint on some lady's coat, just because she doesn't believe like us. That's not Courage, Fellow Fur Fighters; that's cowardly vandalism, and should be treated as such.

After all, it doesn't take much courage to toss some defacing substance on a sixty-year-old lady, then run off, does it? If that's the way we want to display Courage of Conviction, then we need to think of something truly courageous.

Like...hey, I've got it! Let's run down to the truck stop and throw paint on that leather-jacketed motorcycle gang that pulled in this morning. That'll show the world old Neill and Fodrod have Courage of Conviction, won't it, Fred?

Fred? Where'd he go?

Well, unlike Fred, sometimes you can get one of these Fur Fighters to stand still and talk to you about it. I tried that, and this lady says, "The real issue here is the cruel pain and unnatural death of the animal." Hey, I understand pain; I have had too much of that for awhile, and have looked unnatural death right in the eye and shivered. I can be Against that.

But back to logic for a minute: if we're going to be "Agin" pain and unnatural death, we've got to be opposed to all of it, to avoid appearing hypocritical, right?

So, no more steak. No more fish or fowl, froglegs, or raw oysters. Tough bananas, Ronald McDonald and Colonel Sanders. We're headed down to the VeggieWeggie for a cheese-broccoli-burger.

Whoa; wait a minute. Broccoli is cut from a living, growing plant. Scientists have now discovered that plants also experience pain, even screaming "Eeekk! Eeekk!" when pulled from the garden rows. We're "Agin" pain and unnatural death, remember? Broccoli is out. Also okra, lettuce, turnip greens, fried green tomatos, and corn on the cob. Veggies must die a natural death before we non-hypocritical Fur Fighters will touch them. So, what's on our menu?

Bread's okay, since the wheat and oats die naturally before being harvested. Jelly's fine, as long as we're waiting until the plums fall before making it. Most fruit and nuts, after they hit the ground, can be judged dead naturally. Grits is good, and cornbread, as is popcorn; kernals of corn are finished when they're hard. Hey, what if the chickens and cows die of old age? Can we eat those *old* drumsticks and ribeyes? Wear leather jackets made from *old* cows? What about naturally gray mink coats, then?

I'm having a hard time understanding our principles here, Fellow Fur Fighters.

If a living tree was cut down and sawed into boards to make the banker's new house, isn't it okay for me and Freddy Fodrod to toss red paint on his walls to protest pain and unnatural death? C'mon, Fred, let's run...durn, he was here a minute ago!

Maybe he went down to the pool hall...but, come to think of it, he wouldn't do that. Aren't billiard balls made from ivory that comes from dead elephants? Having brought that up, aren't piano keys made from the stuff, too? Here, Betsy, throw out those Ferrante and Teicher tapes! We got Principles!

Seriously, people are sure hard to figure out sometimes. Reminds me of that joke about the "Fers" and "Agins" in the old country church. Someone had made a good crop and donated a goodly sum to the Lord's House, and the deacons were meeting to try to decide what to spend it on. One of the "Fers" stood and announced, "I'm fer gittin' a chandelier!"

Upon which, an "Agin" jumped to his feet and declared, "Well, I'm agin that!"

"How come?" the preacher asked.

"Well, I'm agin it fer three reasons: fust, we ain't got nobody kin spell it; second, we ain't got nobody kin play one; and third, we really need more light in this church!"

Seems like a lot of people in this old world are just always "Agin" something, no matter whether they know anything about it. What we really need, in my opinion, are more "Fers."

Instead of making a fool or criminal of yourself by throwing paint on a lady's fur coat, why not work for the preservation of wetlands, so that furbearers will be able to return to their natural range and habitat?

Instead of railing about the occasional leopardskin coat, ally yourself with an international organization striving to organize game laws and protection in Africa, a continent in which political unrest and poaching, not sport hunting, have placed many species on the endangered list.

Instead of griping about Americans eating steak, fish and chicken, promote the shipping of surplus food to the folks starving because of the encroaching Sahara Desert, then spend your money to make sure that food actually gets to the people who need it instead of some penny-ante dictator's terrorist army.

If you must be "Agin" something, for God's sake don't waste your time being Against my gloves and shoes. Be Against drugs, drunk driving, acid rain, and disappearing wildlife habitat. Be Against abortion, terrorism, and organized crime. Be Against profanity and immoral behavior on primetime television, or the pollution of our environment.

Yet—why can't we all be "Fers"?

Instead of being Against abortion and teenage pregnancies, why can't we be For good old-fashioned chastity—both boys and girls!—until marriage? Why not get high on Jesus instead of marijuana, cocaine, and beer? Stand strong For Designated Drivers. Does the manufacture of whatever plastic coat you're wearing cause holes in the ozone layer? Or worsen the Greenhouse Effect? Maybe being "Fer" leather jackets isn't so bad, after all.

Heckfire, if you really like onions, stand up and be counted! Just don't expect me to kiss you right after supper.

I'll have catsup on my steak, please. I'm For that.

THE ELIXIR OF LIFE

I've always heard the old saying "What goes around comes around," and I've seen it happen time and again. I thought about it the other morning, when my son got up before I did for a turkey hunt. My alarm had not yet gone off when I sniffed a wonderful odor from the kitchen. The boy was making coffee for his old daddy!

I had been just about his age when my old daddy had taught me to make coffee, ostensibly so I could bring him a cup in bed on hunting camp. Twenty-five years later, I was now realizing that it was not the cup of coffee in bed that Big Robert desired so much as the *smell* of the black brew to wake up to.

I am aware that modern technology has provided us with timers on coffee makers, so that you can build your coffee the night before to wake up to the next morning. However, I am partial to boiled coffee: the *real* stuff, with grounds in the bottom of the pot, some of which pour into your cup so that you dare not drink the final swallow. Coffee that you dare not leave a spoon in too long. Coffee that has enough "sumption" to hold its heat like a brick from the hearth. That's coffee that's good to the last bite!

Boiled coffee—my mother-in-law, Miss Mable, used to say—should only be stirred with a green stick. You boil the water, pour it over the grounds in the pot, let it boil up, remove the pot and stir it down, do that three times, then run a cup of cold water down the spout to settle the grounds. Only thing is, all of the grounds fail to settle, and some come out into each cup. And that's all right; it's kind of like ashes on a hot dog: part of our culture. Down Here, we just make allowance for that.

But we need to warn folks from other parts of the country sometimes. I mean, they've not been Raised Right. Twice recently, I've served coffee to non-Southerners, and forgotten (really!) to tell them not to drink that last swallow. Both times, they obviously confused the grounds in their mouth with spent chewing tobacco, or something. It was a very traumatic experience for both of them. I almost felt sorry.

But it never would have happened had our nation not strayed from one of our basic American creeds: strong black coffee!

After all, they threw the tea overboard, remember?

In the past few years, the coffee industry has come out with decaffeinated coffee. With all due respect, as far as most outdoorsmen are concerned this is like having turkey and dressing without the turkey; ham and eggs without the ham; peaches and cream without the peaches; bourbon and water without the bourbon. The last thing a hunter needs is to fall asleep when that big old gobbler who shut up an hour ago comes slipping in from behind!

A few weeks ago, I had the pleasure of an overnight visit with friends who don't drink coffee, though otherwise they're very nice folks.

That next morning, the man of the house hunted up some old instant decaffeinated coffee. (That's a real misnomer, isn't it? Kinda like saying de-gunpowdered shotgun shells!) Jim mixed me up some of the stuff with hot water and served it apologetically.

Which was certainly the right attitude.

In the first place, I could see the bottom of the cup, even when it was full. That's what we call "minnow coffee" in Mississippi: if there had been a minnow in the cup, I could have seen it swimming all the way down to the bottom! But I was Raised Right, so I politely and dutifully took a sip.

Try this: while you're enjoying your morning shower, just open your mouth under the nozzle and guzzle some. If you've got it adjusted to fine spray, that will be more stimulating than my coffee that morning.

Coffee *belongs* to be invigorating: to have a kick. That rich, brownish, slightly tangy, faintly earthy smell that neither rises nor falls, but hovers at shoulder level throughout the house, gives one a reason to start the day. Even if today happens to be the day they're foreclosing on your family home, or the day you're scheduled for hemorrhoid surgery, for just a little while you can experience the sheer pleasure of hovering over that first cup of black brew. I love the smell of caffeine in the morning!

In his book *Tenth Legion*, Alabaman Tom Kelly declares that the Confederate Army performed the greatest feat known to military history by surviving four years of war on a brew of ground roast acorns as a substitute for coffee. No doubt that concoction was also decaffeinated, just like the stuff that had sat in Jim's cupboard for so long. Heck, I don't care a thing about hunting, fishing, or anything else for that matter, without my morning coffee. I'd hate to even think about having to get up and shoot yankees after a cup of acorn juice.

Have you ever thought about the fact that the Dark Ages ended and the Renaissance began when

Christopher Columbus discovered America...and coffee?

SOMETIMES YOU DO SHOOT THE LADIES, AND DON'T HAVE TO LIE ABOUT IT

An acquaintance of mine was doing a little bragging recently about the turkey he had killed last season. "Sucker had a ten inch beard!" he informed the group. One of his audience wanted some elaboration, and began asking about weight, length of spurs, whether the bird was strutting or gobbling, and other usual particulars. The hunter seemed remarkably eager to let someone else brag on their turkeys, but the questioner obviously knew more than he was letting on. Turned out that the turkey in question had been that rare oddity, a bearded hen; and the bragger had not bagged a gobbler to expound upon that season.

Having once brought in a bearded hen myself, I sympathized with the storyteller, but joined in the fun at his forced admission. Of course, it was an honest mistake, and thereby forgivable, yet not braggable-on. Unless one was to lie about it, that is.

Sometimes one doesn't have to lie to give a false impression. I remember one time when some of us Ole Miss fraternity brothers had been invited to participate in a doe hunt on an island where the deer population had built up to the danger level. As most sportsmen know, game populations on limited acreages must be controlled, or else disease and starvation will set in. Mother Nature can be

236

cruel, too, and mankind is Biblically obligated to pay attention to game management. In this case, biologists had recommended taking off a goodly number of does to prevent a die-off situation.

I don't know what the anti-hunting folks think happens when habitat gets overpopulated. Most states can't even afford to pay what game wardens they have, and trapping for relocation costs money that usually isn't in the budget. Hey, I've seen die-offs, and they don't discriminate. Bambi dies just as dead from starvation as a well-placed bullet, he just suffers a lot longer. And even worse than seeing a die-off is...smelling one!

Believe me, once you've smelled death whole-sale like that, you understand a little better when the biologist says to take off a certain number of does.

The island in question was in another state, and we were on our way home with a pickup load of deer—all legal—when we stopped for gas. Mom Raines was closest to the pump, and the attendant engaged him in conversation as he was filling the tank. It was a classic case of false impression with nary a falsehood.

The attendant raised his eyebrows at the stacked deer (there were a half-dozen of us, and the limit was two apiece). "Y'all been huntin', have ya?" he asked.

Mom considered a moment before replying, then nodded. "Yeah, we have been huntin'. Sho' have!"

The attendant tried again, his curiosity obviously piqued, for deer season was closed in his state, which we had to cross on our way home. "Been deer huntin', I reckon?"

Mom sucked a tooth for a moment, as the rest of us let him carry the ball. Finally, he nodded again, "Well, yeah, we have been doin' a little deer huntin'."

"Looks like y'all had a little luck," was the next observation, as the guy eyed the mound of deer.

Again Mom nodded, close-mouthed. "Little bit," he agreed.

The man loosened his grip on the pump handle, as the tank began making bubbly-filled sounds. "I didn't realize deer season was still open around here. Y'all must have special licenses."

At that Mom raised an eyebrow. "Y'all gotta have a license to hunt deer in this state?" he asked in a surprised tone.

Now the attendant was working himself up. "Why, heck yeah, you gotta have a license! And the season's been closed for three weeks, too!"

Mom shook his head in obvious disgust at the interference of government with man's enjoyment of nature's bounty, while I paid the man and got back in the truck. "Well, all that stuff don't make no difference anyways," he informed the gaping attendant. "We ain't got nothin' but does!"

The guy was dialing the telephone as we left the filling station. I'm sure some game warden got an earfull!

MAMA, DON'T SEND YOUR JAKES
TO WAR!!
(Written In August, 1990)

"Oh, boy!" the young man exclaimed, "We're gonna go to war. I bet we'll get to go in and kick tail and take names! We'll be T-U-Double-Uff Tough! It'll be like deer season on the sand dunes!" This was a typical Jake: a young, immature male turkey!

But the deer don't shoot back, I told him.

Throughout the ages, poets and writers have glorified war, and it ain't so. Oh, there are plenty of writings to the effect that "War is hell," to quote a yankee general, but often these are taken as traitorous, or at least unpatriotic, statements, and thereby discounted as the wimpish ramblings of some liberal left-wing communistic pinko. Real Men charge machine gun nests with a pistol in one hand, a grenade in the other, and a knife in their teeth. And the bad guys are sore afraid, and miss every shot.

Maybe. And maybe young men who are crack marksmen, expert woodsmen, and blood kin to Davy Crockett will triumph over the devil himself before football season starts. That kind of thing happens on half the tapes in the video store. But don't count on it happening to your Jakes, Mama.

One of the finest young hunters I ever hope to know died in a jungle a long way from home. Two other long-time outdoor companions were badly wounded. The ability to make oneself a part of nature isn't really an advantage to a young man in a shooting war; matter of fact, it generally insures that the kid will quickly be elevated to the position of point man, which places him in even more danger. Or, as a typical Jake might put it, more opportunities for glory. Kick tail and take names!

Please don't misunderstand me here: I'm more patriotic than most folks, and I'm teetotally in favor of kicking tail when we have to, as a nation or personally. I've been shot at in combat and have returned fire. Maybe I've killed for my country. But I was abso-dam-lutely terrified when fifty-caliber tracer rounds seemed to be homing in on my position, and remember thinking at the time that I'd rather be home with my wife and kid.

We may have to go to war to get the price of gasoline back down to a reasonable level. We may be obligated to go to war to honor solemn treaties and commitments. We may need to go to war to keep some power-crazed madman from wrecking the globe. We may even have to go to war to protect our country, our family, and our Way of Life.

But rest assured—it ain't gonna be fun. It's not like an extended turkey season with unlimited bag limits.

It's no fun to drag the bleeding, moaning body of a guy you ate supper with off of a chopper. It's no fun to see coffins containing young friends lowered into the ground. It's no fun to watch buddies learn how to walk again. I even lost my appetite for steaks once, when we had to use the "reefers"—the refrigerated compartments of the ship—to store dead Marines. After mustering a working party to restack nineteen full body bags so that the cooks could get to the steaks, I went on a diet of grits for a week. No glory there. War is hell.

I understand that armies are needed. I understand that there are times when one has to fight. I think that heroes are a glorious part of our heritage, and courage is a wonderful trait.

But I also hold to the words of a character from *THE JAKES!*: "I've got two rules about fightin': Number one, don't fight; and Number two, don't fight fair!"

Mr. President, if we have to fight a war, then please fight it like one of those youngsters was your Jake. This country has spent many bazillion bucks to develop weapons that will kill from afar; that will teach the bad guys a lesson—nay, even totally eliminate the bad guys—without endangering one single American serviceman. I'm not talking Hiroshima or Nagasaki; I'm just saying a simple surgical strike using all this fantastic technology we've developed, in lieu of sacrificing Jakes who don't know war is sweat and blood and guts and tears and terror and pain and screaming and death. And courage, glory, and honor too; I'll admit that.

No more Walls, Mr. President. Kick tail and take names, if we must, but don't build any more big, black, granite Walls. Blow up the bad guy's favorite deer camp, or his harem, or his swimming pool with him in it. Just a simple message: if you do this, we'll do that. But leave us our Jakes, Sir.

God love 'em, they don't know enough to be terrified of war.

It ain't fun.

Mom

Teddy

S.P.

Ronny

HOLIDAYS AND OUTDOORSMEN

I'm not going to sit here and try to make the claim that outdoors people have a better handle on religion than most folks. But I will claim that they have a better appreciation of most holidays. It's long been a custom among outdoorsmen to dove hunt on Labor Day, deer or quail hunt on Thanksgiving, duck or deer hunt throughout the Christmas/New Year season, turkey hunt on Easter, and barbeque at the lake on the Fofa July.

Outdoorsmen therefore look forward to holidays with more enthusiasm and fervor than even preachers (who, after all, have to work during all these celebrations!). Often we get accused of neglecting the holiday for the hunting, and that's really understandable, but hopefully not true. I'd like to think that the people who spend a lot of time with nature as God made it are actually able to see the Creator a little clearer than most.

But, as I said to begin with, I ain't gonna make that claim wholesale. Yet I would like to give you a glance at some of the outdoor holiday perspective, from the Brownspur angle anyway.

HOLIDAYS AND CALORIES

A college roommate's mother had passed away, and I went up for the funeral. Afterwards, we were sitting around S.P.'s house reminiscing, drinking coffee, and eating some really delicious teacakes, when his wife came in and eyed the fast-disappearing mound on the plate. "Better watch your calories; you know what they do to your blood pressure!" (Old college roomies are bad to develop the high blood.) "Folks have brought all these cakes and pies, and this is right before Thanksgiving; then you're going hunting, and then comes Christmas. Don't eat yourself to death before New Year's."

Well, I did what good friends are supposed to do in situations like this: I went right to the Bible.

"The Good Book declares that there are no calories in food brought by friends for funerals," I told Charlotte. "Same holds for any religious holiday, or the Fofa July; Book of Bob 6:14" The lady was rather skeptical at first, but S.P. and I were finally successful in convincing her to join us before the teacakes got wiped out. As she sipped and nibbled also, I amplified my original point.

You see, there isn't a lot that folks can actually do to show their sympathy, or empathy, when someone dies. In the South especially, it has become a custom to take a dish over to the house as a tangible show of love, knowing that the family and friends will descend for several days. Teacakes, lemon meringue pie, or even banana pudding prepared with this type concern is totally devoid of calories, cholesterol, or anything else considered bad for old college roommates.

244

Same holds true for Thanksgiving, Christmas, and Easter. Any parent of a college student can testify that if such meals contained calories, said student would roll back to classes instead of walking. Science has not yet developed an intake meter capable of measuring the Christmas capacity of a typical college junior. I think the problem is that present meters are calibrated in pounds instead of tons. Three college athletes home for five days of deer hunting and holiday meals will consume more food than the entire Confederate Army did during the whole Vicksburg siege.

When we all get to Heaven, it will be revealed to us that men go to hunting camp to eat; yet many men actually lose weight at camp. Dieticians are just now beginning to catch on to the fact that venison, duck, wild hog, cathead biscuits, and sorghum molasses register negative readings on calorie and cholesterol scales, if consumed at least six miles from a corporate limit. Two-inch-thick beefsteaks grilled in the woods are not only good, but good for you, and the dessert of fruitcake and coffee with Khalua is quite healthy if one is sitting around a campfire.

Now, double-creme Oreos and beer soda would be worth five pounds an hour while watching a football game, but doesn't count against you atall if consumed during an afternoon in a fishing boat. Sardines, crackers, rat-trap cheese, gingersnaps, and any bellywarsh worthy of the name are not only non-caloric, but would restore the USA to Olympic supremacy if prescribed as a training diet for our athletes. If scientists were to check, they would find that there's not nearly as much power and energy in ten pounds of steroids as there is in three cans of flat sardines.

245

There's power in those little fishes that could change the world, if used by the right people. I was in Washington, D.C. once to meet with some of the high muckety-mucks about the farm crisis, and they took me to lunch at the Press Club. Instead of having a good ole "jungle-lunch" and going back to work, we ate something called "orange roughy" (which S.P. said sounded fishy) with a sauce I couldn't pronounce, and side dishes of asparagus, brussels sprouts, boiled carrots, and white wine. Can you see them going back to the Hallowed Halls and considering world-changing legislation after a meal like that? Maybe we've stumbled onto one of the basic problems in our country today. Not to mention the root of the budget problem, S.P. pointed out.

You never see any skinny folks in Washington, unless it's those like "yon Cassius, who have that lean and hongry look."

And as for all those government giveaway programs, wonder if they're aware that it was undoubtedly three cans of flat sardines that Jesus fed the 5,000 with? A few of these well-applied Christian principles could solve a lot of problems, just as it solved the problem of a too-full plate of teacakes the day Mama Nell was buried.

One must be careful to stick to the good old conservative King James Version on this topic, I must warn you. Some of the newer translations seem to indicate that wedding feasts and family reunions follow this same line of theology, but I have reason to believe these are false prophecies. Statistics show that weddings are only about fifty percent effective, and family reunions less than that. However, funerals and hunting camps are nearly a hundred percent effective, and even

Congress recesses for Thanksgiving, Christmas, Easter, and Fofa July. I mean, did you ever hear a hunter say, "I'm not going back to camp next year"? Would you send your child to a school that didn't schedule Christmas Holidays? See what I mean?

"God's on our side," I assured Charlotte, as S.P. picked up the last teacake. I cast my eye at the lemon icebox pie.

MOTHER'S DAY
(WE LOVE THE LADIES EVERY DAY ANYWAY)

It's just that today, we're supposed to say it out loud.

Us boys aren't real bad about saying it; it's just supposed to be absorbed, like osmosis. Mommas and wives need to hear it now and then, though. I say wives, because it should be a given that mothers are supposed to be wives first, though biologically I know that's not set in stone. And quite frankly, even though it may not be politically popular to admit it, I have an idea that most husbands get about as much mothering as little boys, once they both get past the dirty diaper stage.

Especially husbands and sons who hunt, fish, and engage in outdoor sports. Who has to gather and wash the long johns we've lived in for a week on deer camp? (Matter of fact, that ain't far from the dirty diaper stage, I suspect!) Who has to check pockets of jeans for toad frogs, second-hand chews of tobacco, shotgun shells, deceased (but

247

forgotten!) doves, and other nasty items before said jeans go into the washing machine? Who has to refrain from killing the men who track mud across her living room floor and rugs when they return from duck hunting an hour before her bridge club? Who has to get up at three a.m. to cut off the alarm and wake up her turkey hunters? Who then takes pity on them and goes to the kitchen to make coffee? Who worries herself almost to tears on cold rainy nights when her menfolks are two hours late coming home from duck hunting on the river? Who spends her summer evenings for ten years on bleacher seats eating suppers of cold hot dogs while watching her Little League son star despite the stupid coaches and umpires, either or both of which she could replace quite well?

The mothers and wives of us sporting men and boys, that's who!

Until we had a houseful of JAKES ourselves, I don't think I ever really appreciated what my mother, Miss Janice went through, when I'd show up unexpectedly from college with a half-dozen fraternity brothers for a weekend dove hunt. Not that she, or Betsy, ever minded, for with kids that say "yes ma'am, no ma'am, thank you ma'am, please" or remember birthdays and Christmases or just drop by to say "howdy" now and then for years afterward—in other words, *nice* kids—the association is a pleasure forever.

I mean, at least they were all past the dirty diaper stage!

I'd put my own JAKES up against any other picked team in an eating contest serving venison, doves, duck, and lemon meringue pie. Yet, just watching the food vanish during last Easter Break reminded me of Miss Janice's expression while watching me, Semmes Ross, Mom Raines, Hog Evers, Ronny James, and Fat John Bryan consume the huge roaster of barbequed doves that she had figured would last that whole weekend. We polished it off at one sitting, and still had room for both lemon pies. While Momma had lots of experience in the teenage-boy-appetite field, having gone through my bunch of high school buddies, it was her first table setting of full grown college boys, and she took it as a challenge. By the time we left for Ole Miss on Sunday, she had risen to the occasion, and Ronny even asked to be adopted. Hog was so full, he didn't eat for two days afterward. He's the only one of those guys who doesn't still come by on a regular basis.

I've always been lucky enough to have womenfolks who kept an "open home" policy, and have seen young men come and go for thirty years now. Our home was their home, and they knew it, but didn't abuse it. Ronny and Mom even brought their intendeds by for "approval" by Big Robert and Miss Janice, and it must have taken, because they're both working up on 25th anniversaries. What goes around comes around, and now THE JAKES come in with young ladies for Other Mother to get to know. It's a good feeling, and it's there because of...well, you know...aw, that little ole four-letter word us sporting men hardly ever say...it's...aw, shucks, you know what I mean, don't you?

I think they do know, fellows; they have to get it by osmosis a lot of times, but I think they know.

However, it's okay for us to say it out loud today.

"Love."

THE BEST THANKSGIVING

More than twoscore Thanksgivings get jumbled up in my memory, but in general, the holiday has always been a gathering at someone's home to eat. And eat well, I mean: turkey (usually wild), dressing, cranberry sauce, sweet 'tater casserole, oysters Johnny Reb, homemade wholewheat rolls, and both mince and pecan pie. We're talking major pigout.

What was really terrible was that for many years, deer season opened the very next day, so we menfolks would dine in our hunting clothes. Stuffed to the point of gluttony, we'd rise right after dessert, grab the guns, and head the already-loaded jeep toward the river. However, I was never too full to forget to snag what was left of the pies on the way out.

It made for a better holiday when the powers that be moved deer season up a week.

There were Thanksgivings at grandparents', Thanksgivings at in-laws', Thanksgivings at both old and then new homes as families grew, there was even a Thanksgiving at sea. But perhaps the best Thanksgiving was the one that, crazy as it sounds, I spent in the hospital.

Now, I don't mean it was a fun holiday; far from it. There had been a lot of pain involved; big league pain. Then immobility; flat on my back for a month. The anxiety was even worse than the pain: would I be able to walk again when they finally said to try? Worst of all was being a whole month on a bedpan.

250

Total depression. I mean, a month on a bedpan will depress even a healthy optimist. Here Thanksgiving was approaching, with its accompanying deer season, and I had absolutely nothing for which to be thankful. No doubt I pointed this out to anyone who would stand still long enough to listen. Turkey, dressing, and sweet 'tater casserole have very little attraction to a patient on a bedpan. As the noon dinner hour neared, I withdrew sullenly from the world, envisioning the fun and fellowship everybody else was enjoying. What about pore li'l ole me?

Then in walked my wife, along with an old college roommate and his wife. Betsy had called Gary and Ann to explain the problem and a possible solution. The couple had made the two-hour drive, giving up holidays (and Gary deer season!) with their own families. But sometimes family doesn't necessarily mean blood.

Seems like they did bring something to eat; I think Betsy had fried up some quail. Whatever it was, it was delicious. But the main things they brought were a lap board and a couple of decks of cards. For two days, we played bridge, with all the laughing, talking, and fun that goes on during friendly card games.

It was my first forty-eight hours in four weeks without a pain shot.

Thanksgiving is not the food on the table, or even having a table. Thanksgiving is being thankful for the family and friends that surround you. Having a wife that strives to understand your situation and remedy the problem is something to be thankful for. Having friends that will go to great lengths to help out, even if it means a weekend in a hospital room without inside plumbing; that's what makes a person thankful.

A week later, walking seemed easy after that; but if I hadn't been able to, I'd still have considered myself blessed for a wife and a bunch of friends like that.

Yeah, that was a great Thanksgiving!

SHOULD AULD ACQUAINTANCE BE FORGOT

Dear All Y'All,

As New Year's of 1991 approaches, I've had occasion to think a little more than normal about The Old Dove Season Bunch. You realize it's been thirty years since most of us entered Ole Miss together? I met Semmes before anyone else, because freshman football players had to be at school three weeks before the rest of the class. Our hair was already growing back when y'all showed up that fall of 1960.

Thirty years! Lord, where have they gone? Seems like only yesterday that we all piled into the old hearse and y'all came home with me for your first time on Opening Day of Dove Season. The Party was held at Uncle Sam's house back then. Within five years our Bunch had grown to the point that we started our own Party, then our elders started partying with us soon thereafter. That was the year the cops came and asked us to quiet down. Ann and Betsy were playing "The Impossible Dream" for Semmes and me to sing—at two a.m.! (the cop pointed out.) Who would have dreamed we'd still be singing songs at Dove Season? Except that now the Dove Season Choir is partly composed of JAKES.

Well, 1990 was one heckuva year for the ODSB.

I was visiting at Mom and Linda Raines' last month when Mom hit the Big Five-O, which was only a week or so after Ronny James became the first ODSB grandpa, at least as far as I know. And y'all remember that at Dove Season we announced that Ted had suffered a light heart attack, and did a special prayer for him. Last weekend the first JAKE got married, Clif, with a couple more not too far behind, apparently.

On the other hand, both Semmes and S.P. have kids who will start kindergarten next year. I'm glad it's them and not me.

Admiral Drake, Mountain Willy, Dude, and I have all undergone drastic career changes in the past year or so, and Dude's required him to be in New York City during most of Duck Season. Is that a shock, or what? Gary and Ann have finally gotten settled back in their native Arkansas, but without most of their accumulated stuff of a quarter century of marriage, which the moving company saw fit to burn. Mick has relocated here from Colorado.

Betsy and I, and Beau, were some of the first to lose our parents, but time is beginning to take its toll of many of our forebears: Russ, S.P., Gary, and Gene have all lost parents in the past year or so, and several other parents have suffered stokes or serious illness.

In spite of being married to Doctor Fred (this year's Turkey Award winner), Barbara developed bad back trouble. My anemia came back when the

Lyme Disease left, and S.P. has the high blood. Semmes, on the other hand, lost about a hundred pounds (me and Dude found it!), and Admiral Drake lost back down to fighting weight. Fred broke his ankle jogging to keep weight off. Ted dropped a bunch after his attack. Beau never had the problem, durnit. Even as a JAKE, he was slim.

Two of the past three Opening Day Parties, the Turkey Awards have gone to JAKES. And they have, for all practical purposes, been running the hunt itself for three years. It's been nice, in a way, to kick back and let them handle the load, but on the other hand, I look at our own assorted potguts, bald heads, eyeglasses, and physical deficiencies and wonder, "Are the youngsters doing all this because they *want* to, or *have* to?"

And then the last straw: THE JAKES were all sitting around after Dove Season, reminiscing, and one of them remarked, "Y'all realize that we're getting old?"

If THE JAKES are old, what are we?

I love you Old Dove Season Bunch anyway. Happy New Year, you old geezers. Thanks for all the memories.

Semmes

Gary

THE JAKES' NIGHT BEFORE CHRISTMAS

Twas the night before Christmas, and down in the den
The boys were discussing what Santa might send.

"My old fishing reel backlashes every third cast,"
Tom said, "I'd like something to help me catch bass."

Bryon chuckled,"Way you fish, a dynamite case
Would be better than Garcia's new Open Face!"

"I'd like a new rifle," Joe said, "Old one misses!"
"Ten times at one buck ain't the gun!" Mark insisted.

"Shotgun shells," stressed Adam. "I've shot all I had."
"Plus your dad's, Uncle Beau's, and mine!" Guy shook
     his head.

Mark wished for a scope "That'd miss no more deer."
"Grenades won't help you!" Coo joked with a jeer.

As the boys were discoursing, they did not suspect
That Santa was listening outside on the deck.

"These kids are unreal!" St. Nick said with a shake.
"They must think ole Santa's bread ain't quite baked!"

"Guns, knives, and shells! Let's be on our way!"
And Santa Claus vaulted back into his sleigh.

But Rudolph the Red-Nosed stomped with his hoof.
"Hey, Santa, you done left your mind on the roof!"

"Remember that white house back down the block?
That guy wanted condoms to fill up his sock!"

"And not even married!" Cupid spoke with a snort.
"Like that girl on Third street who just had to abort!"

Blitzen cried, "You left gifts where we saw all that smoke!
'Cept it was marijuana, not hickory or oak!"

Quoth Donner, "That kid whom you gave the new car,
Had smashed up his Olds driving drunk from the bar!"

"These boys are out there in the woods every day.
They eat what they shoot, and they hunt with fair play."

"They obey the laws (oh, they might stretch a limit!)
But they'd turn in a nightshooter quick as a minute!"

Dasher vowed, "They're not out chasing girls in fast cars.
They might DRINK a Coke, but not snort it in bars!"

Santa sheepishly tugged at his beard oh so white,
"Well, deers, you have opened my eyes up this night!"

And grabbing his bag, down the chimney he jumped;
Careful that Mark's Magic Scope not get bumped.

He left guns and shells, skinning knives, hunting britches;
And resolved he'd leave bad kids just ashes and switches.

Then he jumped in the sleigh, and they swept past the front,
Calling,"God bless you boys, and to all a good hunt!!!"

THE CHRISTMAS KNIFE;
A GENERATION LATER

Betsy answered the phone while I was cutting up a buck last week, and it was for me from Charlie Flood, my yankee friend in the north. I was right in the middle of steaking a hindquarter, blood all over my hands, so I asked her to just relay the conversation. At one point, I thought I disagreed with Charlie, and began to hold forth, gesturing with the knife in my hand toward Betsy, who was trying to transmit words and gestures across the telephone lines. Turned out we agreed after all, it was just a language difference. Betsy stopped me in mid-gesture.

I was left staring at the knife in my hand, re-focusing on the familiar object while she and Charlie got things settled without my pontification. Durn, that was an old knife!

Beau had given it to me as a joke Christmas present right after Mom Raines had broken the blade off my hot-shot stainless steel hunting knife cutting a sapling to haul our deer out of the woods. That was about the first-ever doe hunt on our club, and Mom and I had both gotten big mommas, while Ronny James had taken one that Big Robert forever after referred to as "Ronny's baking size doe." When I fumed over the "unbreakable" knife breaking, Beau got me a heavy, inexpensive scabbard knife down at Joe Turner Hardware, wrapped with a note to the effect that maybe even Mom couldn't break this one.

That had been at least twenty-seven years ago, maybe more. My Beau Knife has been my only scabbard knife since then. As I looked closely at the blade, I realized that it was only a little over half as thick as it had been originally. Nearly thirty years of whetrocks, diamond stones, and ceramic sharpeners had taken a toll! A knife is of little use when dull, and this one had always held an edge well. The first trip Gary Dye ever took to the island, this knife had field-dressed five deer in one morning without being whetted. Two for Gary, two for me, and one for Scooter Smith, who was hoss-riding that day.

If I'm not badly mistaken, this knife had also dressed out the last deer Big Robert ever took off Woodstock Island, that big nine-point on the brushy slough behind Dub's Old House. And now that I think about it, probably the last buck he killed on Montgomery Island, too. That was the one he crippled, and Tut Payne finished it off with a John Wayne-type shot from the back of a running horse. Hit the deer right in the neck.

The day that S.P. Crockett killed the little five-point while David Steen and I watched, thinking S.P. was shooting at the big ten-point, I had this knife and used it to help dress out the buck. S.P. had never even seen the big deer, and David and I had been convinced he had shot a doe when the ten-point ran off.

Betsy's first buck, a nine-point, had been field-dressed with this same knife. Johnny Grassi, at the Food Bank, had been a witness when I blooded Betsy's face in congratulatory tradition. He told me later on, "I thought that little gal was gonna skin *you* alive when you slopped that handful of blood on her face!" In obvious admiration, Johnny refused to charge for his butchering on that particular deer.

Adam's first turkey was drawn with my Beau Knife, but his first deer had been field-dressed by Uncle Beau himself, who had shown up right after the kid's shot. I was just out of a knee cast at the time, grateful for little brother's help and knife.

Dude's first deer on the island, Mick's first buck after his return from 'Nam, Neel's and Mark's first ducks, Ted's first turkey, Ranny's wild boar—all gutted with my knife. We cut up for the freezer Joe's and Robert's first bucks with Beau Knife; those two were inspiration for the Rookie character in *THE JAKES!*. When Adam brought his Connecticut teammates, Jake and Joe, for a big rabbit hunt and Jake broke the stock on French Gun, we cut those rabbits up with this knife. The last deer Uncle Sam ever killed, Vernon Skelton and I had gutted with this knife.

It has even performed in non-hunting causes. The day that Beau and I happened upon the little car that had been wrecked, and the young girl's broken leg was jammed in, this knife just happened to be in the truck. Its razor-sharp blade made short work of the knee-high leather boot wedged into the crushed fire-wall, and we had Kim freed before the ambulance arrived.

So, it was a good Christmas present so long ago. But this Christmas, the best thing about that old Beau Knife is the memories it's now wrapped up in. It wasn't a joke after all. And even Mom Raines couldn't break it!

YES, VIRGINIA, THERE IS
A DUDE McELWEE

I have often been asked, both by letter and in person, "Is there really a Dude McElwee, or is he just another figment of your imagination?" Finally, it has reached the point that the man's wife herself, a lady by the name of Virginia, has begun to doubt the existence of said Dude. This being the season that it is (hunting), I thought it best to set the matter straight, once and for all.

Yes, Virginia, there is a Dude McElwee!

He is not exclusively ours, you must understand; he exists in all the friendships formed by those men who answer the call of the outdoors. He is the guy with extra cartridges, when you have left your own in the car three miles away across the levee. He is the one who volunteers to cook supper and wash dishes though you are both bone-tired from a day afield after deer or ducks. He is the only man in camp with a bottle of Khalua for the coffee around the campfire on the day your waders sprung a leak, and you are the only man he'll share it with. He always has at least two of whatever the fish are biting, and loans one to you.

I realize that sometimes such legendary figures become distorted by time and their own statue, yet we must never cease to believe. No doubt Mrs. Johnny Appleseed went through the same crisis you are now experiencing. No doubt Mrs. Bunyan had moments when she was tempted to tell Paul where he could put that big blue ox. Probably Mrs. Claus gets aggravated at having to feed all those elves and a herd of reindeer for twelve months, for only one night of use. And just imagine how

261

seldom the Tooth Fairy's wife saw him during the Baby Boom years!

But we must never cease to believe, Virginia.

If there were no Dude McElwees, why would a man hunt? Certainly the price of dead cow meat is more economical than venison steaks. Oh, some men would continue to roam the woods on an occasional basis just to get away from the telephones, but most would give up the sport. It's the fellowship, the meat grilled over the open fire, the sound of a bobcat's squall that stops a campfire conversation—that's why we go to the woods, most of us. And there must be someone to share it with, whether his name is Dude McElwee, Gary Dye, Beau Neill, or Freddy Fodrod.

Yes, Virginia, there is a Dude McElwee in every sportsman's life. He really does have special powers: he can transform that six-pound bass you caught into a seven-pounder after only two toddies by the fire that night; he can miraculously forget— and thereby erase forever—those four shots you missed at a ten-point standing broadside in the edge of the willow brake; he can wipe away your sorry performance on that last flock of mallards by insisting that he only shot twice, so one of those three drakes must be yours. He appears almost by magic to help you field-dress your buck and drag it to the road. He never heard you shoot when you show up at the jeep with an empty gun and no turkey. He can help you claim the limit with less than a box of shells when you are on a big dove hunt with out-of-state business acquaintances.

I would be remiss, however, especially at this season of the year, if I did not observe that his powers, and the powers of other legendary figures, are nothing next to the powers of the Christ Child whose birth we celebrate. Believing in a Dude McElwee may save you a box of shotgun shells after a duck hunt; believing in Jesus Christ will save your soul. Do not confuse these legends with the Savior.

Yet there is a place in our hearts and our lives for Santa Claus, the Easter Bunny, the Tooth Fairy, Paul Bunyan, Pecos Bill, John Wayne, and Dude McElwee—if kept in perspective. Be thankful for and generous with the larger-than-life friends who share your campfires this season. This type relationship does not exist in many fraternities these days, and our macho images and pride forbid us men to use the term "love" in any other connotations than with beautiful women—or possibly Labradors.

Yes, Virginia, there is a Dude McElwee.

Dude